CW01263858

DAM BUILDERS' RAILWAYS
FROM DURHAM'S DALES TO THE BORDER
and linked branch lines of the N.E.R. and N.B.R.

DAM BUILDERS' RAILWAYS
FROM DURHAM'S DALES TO THE BORDER
and linked branch lines of the N.E.R. and N.B.R.
by
Harold D Bowtell

Plateway Press   P.O. Box 973 Brighton BN2 2TG
ISBN 1 871980 19 4

Books by the same Author:
> Over Shap to Carlisle - the Lancaster and Carlisle Railway in the 20th Century
> Rails Through Lakeland :- Workington - Cockermouth - Keswick - Penrith
> *The Dam Builders in the Age of Steam:-*
>> Reservoir Railways of Manchester and the Peak
>> Reservoir Railways of the Yorkshire Pennines
>> Lesser Railways of Bowland Forest and Craven Country
>> Lesser Railways of the Yorkshire Dales

British Library Cataloguing in Publication Data
Bowtell, Harold D.
  Dam Builders' Railways from Durham's
  Dales to the Border: And Linked Branch
  Lines of the N.E.R. and N.B.R.
  I. Title
  385.0942
  ISBN 1 871980 19 4

© Harold D Bowtell 1994

All rights reserved. No part of this publication may be reproduced, stored in a retrieval system, or transmitted, in any form or by any means, electronic, mechanical, photocopying, recording or otherwise, without the prior written permission of the Publisher.

Printed in Great Britain by Postprint, East Harling, Norwich

Book design by Keith Taylorson.
Cover artwork by John Holroyde.
Typesetting by Martin Snow, Intersoft Multimedia.

Front cover illustration: Andrew Barclay 0-4-0WT GREEN is seen at work on the Durham County Water Board's Burnhope system in the early 1930's. *(R T Horne collection)*

Frontispiece: Hudswell Clarke 0-4-0ST FONTBURN poses at the Fontburn site of Tynemouth Corporation in July 1905. *(courtesy Tynemouth Corporation)*

CONTENTS

		Page
	Preface	7
Chapter 1	**Rails in Yorkshire's Northern Dales**	
	Baldersdale - for Tees Valley Water Board	11
	Locomotives in Baldersdale, all 3ft gauge	15
	Lartington and Catcastle - filters and quarries	16
	Long Newton	19
	Grassholme in Lunedale	20
	Locomotives of John Scott at Long Newton and Grassholme, all standard gauge	23
	The Lunedale Whinstone Company (and its 2ft 6in locos)	24
Chapter 2	**Hinterland of the Hartlepools**	29
Chapter 3	**Wearhead and Waskerley moors**	
	Introduction	33
	Waskerley reservoir	33
	Tunstall reservoir	33
	Smiddy Shaw reservoir	33
	Hisehope reservoir	34
	Beldon reservoir	35
	Locomotives on Hisehope construction: John Scott, standard gauge	38
	The Burnhope project (above Wearhead)	41
	Standard gauge locomotives of DCWB, Burnhope	60
	2ft gauge locomotives on DCWB Burnhope project	60
Chapter 4	**Bound for Geltsdale**	71
Chapter 5	**Geltsdale & Castle Carrock - and Carlisle**	75
	Locomotive 3ft gauge of William Kennedy, Geltsdale	80
	The work of Harold Arnold & Son, at Castle Carrock, 1905-09	80
	Locomotives 3ft gauge of Harold Arnold & Son, at Castle Carrock	84
Chapter 6	**By rail to Catcleugh- the Newcastle & Gateshead Water Company in Northumberland, from the Tyne to close on the Border**	
	The project	85
	The pipeline and associated tramways	85
	Main route of the Catcleugh railway	89
	Catcleugh reservoir site and progress, (to completion)	94
	Locomotives on the Catcleugh railway, all 3ft gauge	101
	The early reservoirs and an early loco, 3ft gauge	107
	Whittle Dean filters and associated locomotives, all 3ft gauge	107
Chapter 7	**Fontburn for Tynemouth**	
	The reservoir and origins	113
	The railway connection at Fontburn	116
	Railways and operation on site	119
	Locomotives of Tynemouth Corporation at Fontburn, all 3ft gauge	125
	The Ewesley Lime Works and quarries - and Ritton White House	126
	Locomotives, all standard gauge, of Ewesley Quarry Company	127
	Fontburn Halt and the Rothbury branch of the North British Railway	128
Appendix	**Railways as walkways, and museums of engineering and railways in North East England**	135
	Acknowledgments.	141

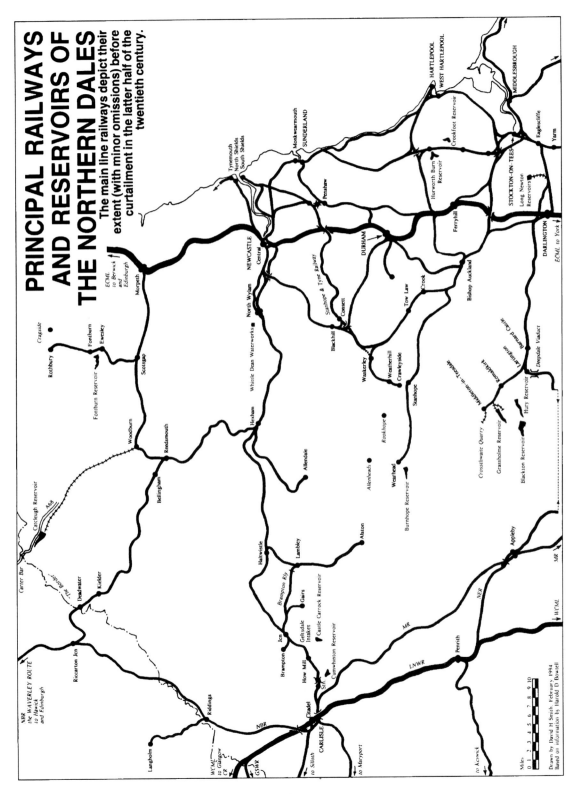

PREFACE

In this, the fifth volume in the series *'The Dam Builders in the Age of Steam'*, I now invite readers to join with me for armchair exploration in Teesdale, on the North Yorkshire/Durham border, and progressively north westward by the dales and Pennine ridges to within sighting distance of the city of Carlisle. Thence, we head northward again to touch (if desired) the Scottish Border at spectacular Carter Bar, taking in Northumbrian villages in the hill valleys of North Tyne, Rede and Font. Some participants in this peregrination will be old friends who have come with me from Manchester's Longdendale dam construction and light railways - in a logical but somewhat devious progression. This is the latest volume in a sequence produced between 1977 and 1994. They tell the story of projects and their people, mainly between 1870 and 1940, with railways, locomotives and steam plant as a common link through the north country dales and moorlands. I know that some of you, after visualising these scenes in my print, diagrams and pictures, have packed your waterproofs and set out to follow the explorations, seeking to advance the derived research. This time, I have set a little puzzle, in Geltsdale (Carlisle's territory) in the book.

All the dams for discussion here are of earthfill construction, involving securing and conveying this bulky material, as well as water-impervious clay to be compacted in the core of each dam. Quarried stone and imported cement have also had to be hauled to the job-sites, plus coal and provisions. Railways on 2ft gauge figure prominently, likewise 3ft gauge and some standard gauge; virtually all those described employed steam locomotives.

These lesser railways had as links and neighbours some of the most delightful branch lines of the old North Eastern Railway - and those by which the North British Railway (with its general manager sitting in Edinburgh) penetrated Northumberland. The general map presented in the book's end covers illustrates my meaning. Likewise, and in some detail, the individual maps and diagrams combine 'main line' Companies' lines with those on the constructional sites; these 'reconstructions' from times past are by cartographer and great friend the late Arthur Chambers. The general map has been lately and specially drawn by David H. Smith. Without straying overmuch from the rugged and ragged site lines, I intend to provide pointers to the connecting trains and traffics of the main line Companies.

Personally, I first came to many of the 'Northern Dales' by cycling over the Pennine ridges from 'railheads' in Settle-Carlisle territory. I well recall darkness descending on the ride from Middleton-in-Teesdale to Weardale; the hill road was more of a track in those days and never - it seemed from the saddle - was the next rise the last before the eventual hairpin descent to the lights of Stanhope. On the same route, but southbound, when a fierce snowstorm blew up, it was happily from the north east.

Even by car, rechecking for the work this year (1993), falling dusk and drifting snow demanded respect.

A 1938 tramp from the up-dale 'bus terminus at Allenheads over the track, now a hill road, by Rookhope Head to the valley of the Rookhope Burn focused attention on the parallel hardships voluntarily endured by the 'guns' of those pre-Range Rover days, sheltered only by the bleak butts when in pursuit of the grouse. From that occasion derived the term 'gricers' for railway enthusiasts seeking remote relics and then-existing lines for leadmines and waterworks in the same moorlands.

This book concludes with acknowledgments, a lengthy roll of names, not all still with us. Let me express special appreciation for substantial help with specific parts of the project - first to John

FOUR WHEELS COUPLED, SPECIAL DESIGN.

Fig. 314. TYPE—" ZURIEL." Code Word—Decupero.

Side Tank Locomotive, with 4 wheels coupled, specially designed for use on inclines, the boiler being fixed at an angle of 1 in 20 so that fire box and tubes are always well covered with water. Suitable for Quarries, Collieries, Iron and Steel Works. etc.

Fitted with front and back sand boxes, rail washers and well protected roomy cab. Square copper fire box and brass tubes. Suitable for gauges of 3′ 6″ to 5′ 6″.

SIZES AND APPROXIMATE SHIPPING PARTICULARS.

Size of cylinders in inches.	Approx. H.P.	Weight in working order. tons.	Code Word.	Packed in one case.		Packed in parts.	
				Gross Weight in cwts.	Measurements.	Heaviest Package in cwts.	Total cubic feet.
8 × 12	60	9¼	Decurvo	170	14′–0″ × 6′–6″ × 7′–9″	78	800
9 × 14	80	12	Decusarlo	230	15′–3″ × 7′–0″ × 8′–0″	82	950
10 × 15	90	15	Decusatori	271	17′–0″ × 8′–0″ × 9′–0″	85	1150
11 × 16½	120	16½	Decusollo			93	1300
12 × 18	145	18	Dedacchia			100	1450

Can be fitted for burning wood fuel, with extra large fire box and wood rack, and can also be made suitable for using oil as fuel. Spark arrester and any type of cab can be fitted to suit special requirements. Other additions and variations to design can be made on receipt of full particulars. For minimum weight of rail recommended and loads engine will haul, see page 4.

WHEN ORDERING USE PRIVATE CODE AT END OF CATALOGUE.

Dawson, who has retired to upper Weardale, in which dale he grew up observantly, with his father a N.E.R. stationmaster. Fred Peadon and his father the late John Peadon have worked with Weardale's water projects for much of their lives. Bob Rennison, a senior engineer in Tyneside water, has himself done vast research on the topic and been ever ready to aid my quest. E.G. (Ned) and Mrs Rutherford of Rothbury have recalled Font valley lore, Ned turning out to point the way. Right through my delvings, help has again constantly come from Allan Baker, Geoff Horsman and Russell Wear. Ken Hoole (who died in 1988) turned up his 'clues' on N.E.R. aspects. His published books develop these themes and his deposited archives are available at the North Road museum in Darlington. By way of appendix, I am adding reference to some of the converted railways which now provide walkways complementary to the routes described in my text.

Harold D. Bowtell

Kendal
Westmorland
December 1993.

Publisher's Note

The books *Reservoir Railways of Manchester and the Peak* and *Reservoir Railways of the Yorkshire Pennines*, both by Harold Bowtell, are out of print. His *Lesser Railways of Bowland Forest and Craven Country* (1988) and *Lesser Railways of the Yorkshire Dales* (1991) can be obtained from Plateway Press or through the book trade.

Reviewers have suggested that each of these books deserves an index but have also accepted that H.D.B. usually leads in with an explicit list of Contents. This time, he has amplified his 'Contents' to point to titles of water authorities and where to find their locomotives tabulated in the pages, also indicating page numbers to locate maps. In the longer term the publisher (supported by the author) would like to produce an overall index for his 'Reservoir Railways'/'Lesser Railways' series; this could offer scope for presenting additional information emerging since the publications first appeared, as well as further illustrations.

It is regretted that copies of photographs featured in the books cannot be supplied to individuals.

Opposite

ZURIEL was supplied by W G Bagnall and Co. Ltd in 1910 for the Lunedale Whinstone Company, and is featured on page 25. Although a very specialised design, Bagnalls nevertheless felt it worthy of inclusion in their 1911 Locomotive Catalogue and, interestingly (as ZURIEL was built to 2ft 6in gauge), describe the type as 'suitable for gauges from 3'6" to 5'6"'.

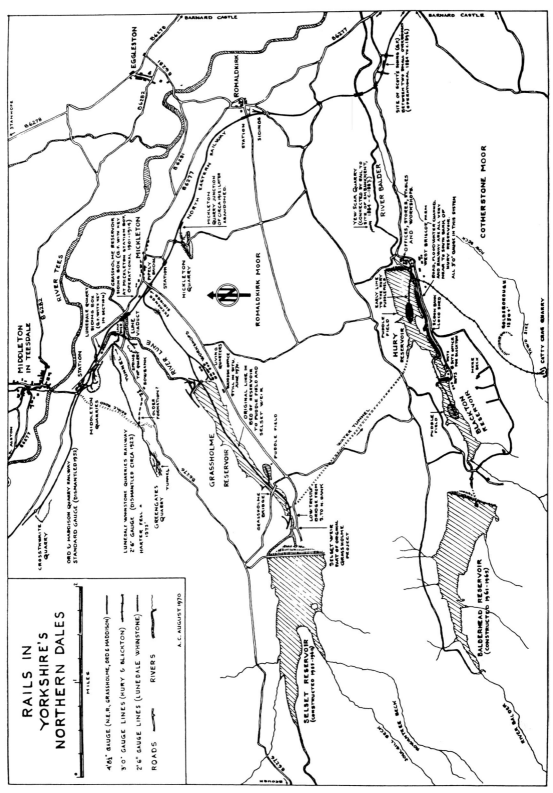

Chapter One

Rails in Yorkshire's Northern Dales

The Setting

Every true railway enthusiast still laments the loss of the North Eastern Railway's cross-country line over wild Stainmore summit, 1370ft.; mineral and goods traffic had already been diverted when the last passenger trains ran on 20 January 1962. Lifting followed, between May 1962 and August 1963. The branch line (opened 12 May 1868) from a delightful terminus at Middleton-in-Teesdale came down from the north west through its village stations of Mickleton, Romaldkirk and Cotherstone to converge with the Stainmore line at Tees Valley Junction, whence the combined route crossed the handsome Tees viaduct— a splendid sight in the evening sun—into County Durham and reached Barnard Castle's newer station, then continuing eastwards to Darlington. The Middleton-in-Teesdale to Darlington diesel passenger units were withdrawn from 30 November 1964 and the line closed entirely from 5 April 1965 back to Forcett Junction (between Barnard Castle and Darlington) and was lifted in 1966. From 2 May 1966 it was abandoned between Forcett Junction and the outskirts of Darlington. The Tees viaduct was demolished in 1971-72.

These were the last railways in Teesdale but they had not been the only ones in those parts. The accompanying maps show 3ft. gauge railways in Baldersdale and standard gauge in Lunedale, waterworks lines which were substantially built and between them spanned the years 1884 to 1914. Traffic reached them by way of the N.E.R. Middleton-in-Teesdale branch.

Baldersdale

The Stockton and Middlesbrough Water Board placed contracts with Walter Scott & Company to build the embankments and other works required to form Hury and Blackton reservoirs in Baldersdale, Hury being the lower and the first to be tackled; the dams were to be respectively 367 and 242 yards long, of earth construction, and the resultant lakes each about a mile in length. A small 'subsidiary reservoir' was to be built between the other two.

The contract for Hury was placed in February 1884, at £112,658.7.9d, and that for Blackton in June 1889, at £118,944. The first sod at Hury site was cut on 14 August 1884. On that occasion a paper on the project was read by W.H.C. Stanford, chief assistant to James Mansergh, the distinguished consulting engineer. Mr Stanford discussed the then known nature of the foundation area across the valley at the site for the dam, the intention being to create a shoe of concrete and fill the trench and embankment core above that entirely with puddle clay, the puddle wall broadening to 22ft at ground level tapering to 6ft thick at its top (at 4ft 6in above top water level). The embankment itself was to rise to about 95ft above the bed of the Balder, with a width at its foot around 550ft and 20ft at the top, giving in practice a water capacity of 859 million gallons. Blackton's capacity proved to be 463 m.g.

A site visit on 30 June 1885 was for the benefit of the North of England Institute of Mining and Mechanical Engineers. John Scott of the contractors gave an outline of the works in progress. Another interesting figure was George Nicholas Yourdi, understood to be of Greek/Irish descent, who was resident superintendent of the Baldersdale works during 1883-1893. He had been resident engineer, Upper Barden, for Bradford, from March 1878 until around 31 December 1882 *(Yorkshire Dales p.73)*. From Hury territory he went on to distinguish himself as resident engineer, Rhayader works, for Birmingham Corporation.

N.E.R. records show that by an agreement of 18 October 1884 with Walter Scott & Company 'Scott's Siding' was put in, 67 chains beyond Cotherstone station and 1 mile 52 chains short of Romaldkirk; the siding was on the north (right hand) side of the single track Middleton-in-Teesdale branch, as seen when proceeding up Teesdale by train. At this point the branch is level with the adjacent land for 100 yards or so,

The scene is Catty Crag quarry, at about 1250ft o.d. on Cotherstone Moor, with derrick cranes, stonemasons and 3ft gauge railway tracks evident. The locomotive is the second ('big') COTHERSTONE 0-6-0 saddle tank with 11in x 17in cylinders, built 1892 by Black Hawthorn of Gateshead and *later* converted to standard gauge.

between two small overbridges giving access to the farmland south of the line. Scott's Siding was built to standard gauge and used primarily for unloading materials. The meadow between the siding and the Baldersdale byroad was used as a base depot and loads of pipes, valves and cement were conveyed from there to the site by horses and carts. The carters had to urge their horses over some two and a half miles of narrow and severely undulating road in days well before the vogue for tar macadam surfaces. The 3ft gauge locomotives, of four and six-coupled types, made their initial journeys to the site at weekends, under their own steam. Four lengths of rail were laid ahead on the road and the locomotive traversed them, horses then hauling the rail lengths ahead again to permit further progress, and so on until the site of Hury embankment was reached. To the right of the road before the present reservoir house were stables for the horses, offices, stores and workshops. The large West Briscoe farm was (and is) a landmark on the left (south) of the road hereabouts. By mid-October 1884 Yew Scar quarry had been opened out, about 900 yards north east of the embankment, and a 3ft gauge railway made to connect it with the site of the contract works, several bridges being involved. The plant then included two locomotives and 94 wagons, so it seems that, if Scott's Siding was not ready, the first locomotives and wagons may have been brought from Cotherstone station yard. Two small second-hand four-wheelers by Hunslet and one by Manning Wardle were the first locomotives.

The Yew Scar quarry had a life of less than three years, being reported closed in September 1887. Meanwhile, in May 1885, a line was completed to Catty Crag quarry and by the following month quarrying was in progress and a locomotive working. This quarry is today an amphitheatre of hewn rock in bleak Cotherstone moor, southwards from Blackton embankment and was reached by two miles of steep line up the slopes of Goldsborough, a rocky outcrop, and over the peat hags to its destination around the 1250ft contour. Following the route is difficult but from time to time one comes upon huge pieces of worked stone and these clearly lie where they fell from the rocking wagons of the contractor over 100 years ago and they confirm the route taken. A photograph is reproduced of the Catty Crag quarry face with

COTHERSTONE in the foreground, this being one of the later six-wheeled locomotives. At the peak of activity two locomotives worked on Catty Crag duties. Loads to and from the quarry ranged up to 18 or 20 of the small contractors' wagons; the first stretch out of the quarry to Goldsborough ridge was steeply uphill and surely the loads would be banked here. After the ridge it would be a matter of brake power!

A puddle-clay site was developed, probably in the reservoir bed, from 1887 and filling of the embankment trench with puddle commenced in August 1887 and was completed about two years later. There is photographic evidence of the usual 3ft gauge side-tipping wagons being moved by horses in this puddlefield and of a steam navvy at work. A view of the Hury embankment nearing full height in 1889 shows two of the small locomotives and two of the six-coupled ones, also the special steam roller by Aveling and Porter, which was used for consolidating the earthwork; this was in service by May 1888 and in July 1888 was reported 'doing better' after alterations to the wheels. It is better seen in the view (1893) of Blackton embankment.

The first sod at Blackton was ceremonially cut by the Mayor of Stockton on 9 September 1889. The railway route, all 3ft gauge, can be seen on the map. It started with the tracks on and about Hury embankment and in front of the reservoir house and skirted the south shore of the lake, soon crossing the permanent floodwater channel, which was constructed between lake and road. The Catty Crag branch here struck off south westwards across channel and road to commence its climb to the quarry and the 'main line' ran on the bank between channel and reservoir. After another half mile there is a promontory into the lake and here, at Scoon Bank, were situated the locomotive sheds. At the head of Hury the line later swung across the subsidiary dam to reach the north shore of the small 'subsidiary reservoir' and came back over Blackton embankment, after throwing off a long spur into the bed of Blackton to a puddle field from which the railway brought clay to Blackton trench. Substantial timber offices and several living huts were

Hury reservoir was constructed 1884-1892. It is seen with house nearly complete and the main embankment well advanced - view southward, in 1889, with two small locomotives and two six-coupled ones, also the special roller by Aveling & Porter.

Blackton construction was during 1889-1896. This is the 'puddle wall' (clay core) seen from the south, in 1892, at about valley floor level, timbered over to protect against flood and frost. In background, excavation extends the trench and future embankment to lock into the valley side. 4 and 6-coupled locomotives have brought 'fill' for discharge to form the embankment and the special roller will consolidate it.

sited near the south end of Blackton bank and men were also billeted in outlying farms. The railway never ran a regular 'Paddy-mail' train and some men walked the ten miles from Barnard Castle and back in the evening; one cannot imagine the workforce of Richard Costain Limited, who built the much larger Balderhead reservoir above Blackton in 1961-1965, walking it daily from 'Barney'.

Hury was filled with water in the autumn of 1892 and by 1893-94 the floodwater channel was well advanced. Blackton was completed in autumn 1896 and filled by the spring of 1897. In October 1896 Scotts removed their huts and plant from Blackton and lifted the railway, concentrating equipment in the yard at Hury. Scott's Siding had disappeared from N.E.R. records by 1 January 1898.

Details of the three small locomotives which started the Baldersdale projects are given below. The old Hunslet BALDERSDALE was prominent later on Enoch Tempest's Walshaw Dean contract, by which time its original name BLACKMOORFOOT was discernible through the worn paintwork. With LITTLE COTHERSTONE it had shared in Pennine reservoir building for Huddersfield Corporation in the early eighteen-seventies, which represented about the first known use of steam 3ft gauge railways in such contract works. The three larger and later locomotives came new from Black Hawthorn of Gateshead around 1885, 1887 and 1891, respectively, and progressively superseded the little engines; in fact, BIG COTHERSTONE (as it was known) of 1891 took the name of LITTLE COTHERSTONE. The locomotive livery was green, with black edging, and set off by brass nameplates; the locomotives were smartly kept.

Lomotives in Baldersdale : 3ft gauge

BALDERSDALE 0-4-0 Saddle tank oc 8 in by 14in
by Hunslet 92 of 1872 - had been new as BLACKMOORFOOT on 24/10/1872 to Huddersfield Corporation Waterworks, being their third locomotive for reservoir construction *(Yorkshire Pennines pp B16-25)*. Huddersfield sold it in 1877 to Benton & Woodiwiss, who were working for Manchester Corporation on waterworks construction near Guide Bridge It may well be that they disposed of it the next year and that it was one of two small Leeds-built locos employed on construction of the 3ft gauge Ballycastle Railway in the north of Ireland (a job of 1/1879 - 9/1880).
It was certainly on Scotts' Baldersdale project - subject of our study - throughout, i.e. from 1883 or 1884, now named BALDERSDALE, until 1894.
This will be the Hunslet 8in loco offered for sale by Walter Scott & Company under address of their nearby Cotherstone office at 28/10/1896.
Enoch Tempest employed it at Bolton Corporation's Molyneux Brow filter beds and then on their substantial Walshaw Dean contract in the Pennines northward of Hebden Bridge *(Yorkshire Pennines B115)*, Tempest ordering a new boiler for the loco in 1/1906.
It appeared by 2/1918 as property of Shanks & McEwan, Scots contractors with diverse interests, often based Mossend way, and gravitated to A.M.Carmichael of Edinburgh, who were using it on the Edinburgh and Glasgow arterial road building of 1924-34 (certainly by 2/1927) and they subsequently had it on the Galloway water power scheme.

COTHERSTONE 0-4-0 Saddle tank oc 8in x 14in
by Hunslet 102 of 1873 - was new as AMALGAMATION to Huddersfield Corporation *(Yorkshire Pennines B25)* and sold thence in 9/1875 to Leeds Corporation for contract work at Swinsty, Fewston and Eccup reservoirs, in turn, *(Yorkshire Dales p.12)*, then for sale early in 1884. Scotts acquired it and renamed it COTHERSTONE for service at Hury and Blackton from circa 1884 until 1891, but it was replaced by a new and larger COTHERSTONE (see below) which arrived in 1/1892 - and it disappears.

LANCASHIRE WITCH 0-4-0 Saddle tank oc 7in x 12in
by Manning Wardle 614 of 1876 - was new 30/6/1876 to Logan & Hemingway, their No.14, at Medbourne (Leicestershire) in construction territory for the Great Northern and London & North Western Joint Railway - thought to have played a part in bridge works; going on (in 1880?) to Braddock & Matthews to work on the improvements, including major re-alignments, of that period for the L&NWR between Bolton and Kenyon Junction; this being essentially the historic Bolton & Leigh Railway route, the loco name LANCASHIRE WITCH of 1828 was applied to this little engine. With this name retained, it was shipped across the Irish Sea in 1884 to work for Walter Scott on building the M.G.W.R.'s obscure branch line from Crossdoney to Killeshandra, near Cavan, coming thence to Baldersdale. The Scotts may first have used it for a year or so on a modest contract for £7,800 for a new reservoir at Winston, between Barnard Castle and Darlington (the lake in Forcett Park?), also undertaken for Stockton & Middlesbrough Water Board. It was a regular performer at Hury and Blackton - and went on afterwards to Walter Scott & Company's contract on the Great Central Railway's new London Extension line and was used in building the approach to Brackley station; then to Walter Scott & Co./Walter Scott & Middleton's construction of standard gauge sidings at Bamford, Derbyshire and the line thence northward for the Derwent Valley Water Board's Derwent Valley waterworks - period here from 5/1901 to about the end of 1902; the line, once built, was worked by the Board with their own standard gauge locomotives. *(Manchester & the Peak pp 69-70.)* This was probably the close of the Witch's career.

MOUNTAINEER 0-6-0 Saddle tank oc 11in x 17in and 2ft 6in dia. wheels
by Black Hawthorn of Gateshead 844 of 1885 - ordered early 1885 for Baldersdale, with specific requirements for a 'strengthened firebox, ashpan and spark arrester'. After its years in Baldersdale, it was converted to standard gauge and used at Catcastle quarry, Lartington and, still as a standard gauge loco, on extension of Middlesbrough dock,

MOUNTAINEER was akin to big COTHERSTONE but the view shows it as converted to run on standard gauge; it worked thus at Catcastle quarry (see text), at Middlesbrough Dock and later again at a Yorkshire colliery.

1901-02, these being John Scott projects. The sojourn at Catcastle may have been after Middlesbrough. Later again, the engine is understood to have belonged to the Low Laithes Colliery Company Ltd., of Wrenthorpe, near Wakefield (and Rawdon?).

NORTHUMBRIA   0-6-0 Saddle tank oc 11in x 17in and 2ft 6in wheels
by Black Hawthorn 926 - ordered 17/11/1887 for eight weeks delivery; there were detail differences from MOUNTAINEER and 'the reversing lever to be so fitted as not to be in anybody's way in getting off loco' - which implies some personal mishap in operation of its predecessor! After Colsterdale, it was on Lartington filters construction, a job which occupied Scotts from 1896 to 1901. I favour this being the loco advertised by J. Scott of contract office, Cotherstone, at High Quarry, Lartington, at 28/11/1900 - but it was converted to standard gauge and transferred to John Scott's Ingleton quarry. Local information secured at Ingleton about 1956 was that the loco arrived at Ingleton in the eighteen-nineties and on closing of the quarry was brought down and broken up at Ingleton - this would be a matter of bringing down the incline and demise near Ingleton LMS(MR) station, in the 1920's.

COTHERSTONE   0-6-0 Saddle tank oc 11in x 17in and 2ft 6in wheels
by Black Hawthorn 1055 - ordered 7/10/1891 for delivery 1/1892 - and to be like the preceding loco - likewise new to Walter Scott & Company, Baldersdale. It was subsequently altered to standard gauge and used on the Middlesbrough dock contract of 1901-02.

Lartington and Catcastle - filters and quarries : also sight of Deepdale

Closely following completion of the Baldersdale scheme came the construction by Scotts of Lartington filter beds, between Cotherstone and Lartington villages. The excavation here was started in the summer of 1896 and work finished in 1901. It was handed over to the Tees Valley Water Board, who had succeeded the Stockton and Middlesbrough Water Board in 1899.

To provide stone for use in these filter beds and subsequently in his dock construction contracts at Middlesbrough (1901-02) and Birkenhead (1906-14) and reservoirs in Lunedale (1901-15), John Scott opened up Catcastle quarry in 1896 - initially it was somewhat anticipatory. The location was above the steep, wooded slopes of the Deepdale Beck, immediately north of the spectacular Deepdale viaduct - one of Thomas Bouch's design - on the Stainmore line. Rail access was at Lartington Quarry Junction box, later known as Lartington West, whence Scott's lines went into the quarry - standard gauge being employed. The siding agreement with the N.E.R. was dated 8 August 1896. It is particularly interesting that, after their work in Baldersdale, Scott converted his three six-coupled Black Hawthorn locomotives from 3ft to

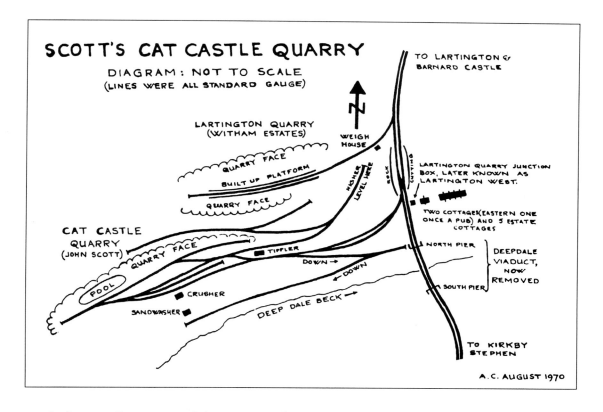

standard gauge. One or two of them were used at the filter beds site, although evidence has proved conflicting as to whether before or after conversion of gauge. NORTHUMBRIA went to Scott's Ingleton quarry, probably in the late 'nineties. COTHERSTONE (the big one) was on the Middlesbrough dock job of 1901-02 and MOUNTAINEER was the most consistent performer at Catcastle quarry. The New Vittoria dock at Birkenhead was finished early in 1914 and around that time Scott finally wound up his quarrying at Catcastle, his siding agreement with the N.E.R. ending 7 October 1914. The course of the zig-zag rail layout there, down to the beck side and up to the quarry top, has been followed in recent years. Bouch's viaduct has been dismantled, shortly after abandonment of the Stainmore line. As viewed in June 1990, the quarries and offices of Cat Castle Quarries Ltd are approached off the road which crosses the former Stainmore line just on the Deepdale (and Kirkby Stephen) side of Lartington station (house). Thus it is much the site as when the siding (or two such) existed just before the first world war.

More on John Scott and contracts

The principal of Walter Scott & Company at the turn of the 19th-20th centuries was Mr John Scott, who lived at Danby Lodge, Darlington and was recalled by near neighbour and industrial historian Ted Haigh as a dapper little man with a 'billy goat' beard, known locally as 'Navvy Scott'. As recently as the summer of 1967, Danby Lodge figured, by kind permission of Lady Starmer, as the location for an ambitious garden party, in aid of charities, with the Newton Aycliffe Silver Prize Band in attendance. Mr John Scott (not, be it noted, Walter Scott & Company) maintained his contact with the Tees Valley Water Board. He tendered for their Grassholme project in Lunedale and associated tunnel, £384,499.14.1d, and for the Long Newton service reservoir contract, £168,062.3.6d. His tenders were accepted on 23 July 1900, and 8 August 1900, respectively.

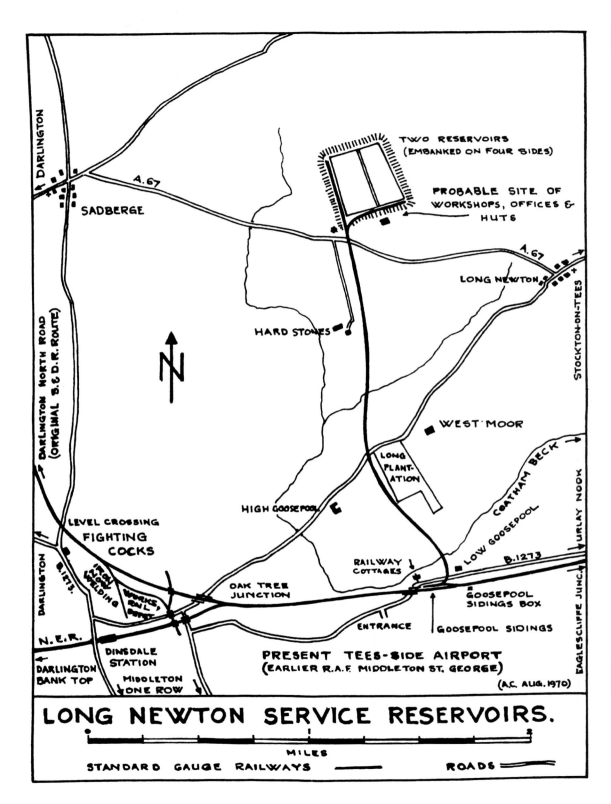

Long Newton - in the flat lands between Stockton and Darlington

Reviewing Long Newton first, storage reservoirs were to be built in the flat agricultural country, midway between Darlington and Stockton, just north of the main east-west A67 road - as it was on my surveys circa 1970, but by 1991 it appears to be A66. The contractor's line, standard gauge, started at Goosepool sidings, about one and a half miles east of Dinsdale station (and less than a mile east of Oak Tree Junction) on the Darlington to Stockton line; this is in the vicinity where the line now skirts the northern edge of Tees-side airport and adjacent to the site of the grandstand erected for the centenary procession (of locomotives and rolling stock) of 1925. The formal siding agreement was dated 20 April 1901 but a connection must have been put in some months earlier. Scott's line swung north over the B1273 (sorry! - now A67) road, then north west to cross the lesser road from Dinsdale to Long Newton, skirting the Long Plantation and almost due north in open country, past Hard Stones farm, over the A67 (no!- A66), already a much widened road by c1970, and onto the contract site, about two miles run from the sidings. The workshops, offices and huts were erected hereabouts. This is a wholly artificial reservoir, excavated and built up with banks on its four sides and a central wall dividing it into two.

The Goosepool and Long Newton line was quickly finished and by February 1901 Scott was laying in tramways of about 2ft gauge on the site itself, probably to assist in the excavation of the bed and the getting of puddle clay. Although work on the job itself started early in 1901, including a puddle trench, by May it was largely suspended due to trouble with sandbeds. The design was altered and a concrete construction adopted, starting in earnest in January 1902. Work then progressed steadily to completion of the outer walls and division wall by about the end of 1904. A ceremonial opening of the main valve was in September

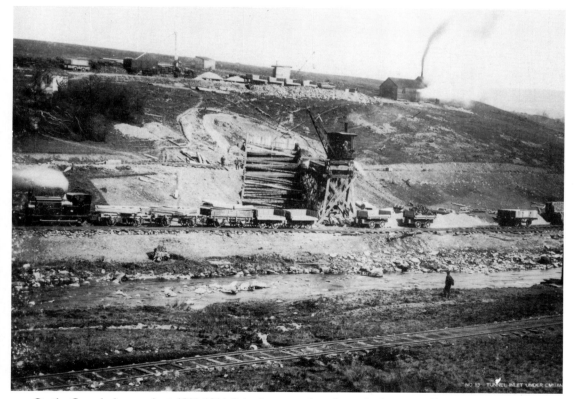

On the Grassholme project, 1901-1914, John Scott employed standard gauge railways. Here, 29 April 1902, early days, the view is believed to look south and is titled 'tunnel inlet under embankment'. Loco DARLINGTON.

1905 by Lady Bell; Bell Brothers ironworks, now long vanished, was then in full operation at Port Clarence and its principals were of the Tees-side hierarchy. The Marchioness of Londonderry was also present at the ceremony, maybe unaware of the number of pheasants caught by locomen and others during their progress through the Londonderry farms and woodlands between Goosepool and the site.

The railway brought in nearly 250,000 tons of materials during its four or five years of activity; materials would mainly comprise cement and also slag from nearby Dinsdale ironworks to reinforce the reservoir bed to a thickness of 15 or 16 inches. Staffordshire blue bricks were brought in to face the dividing wall. Standard gauge locomotives numbered two or possibly three. New inside cylinder 0-6-0 saddle tanks TEES VALLEY and MIDDLESBROUGH (details of which are given subsequently) were delivered by Manning Wardle of Leeds to Goosepool sidings in 1903. A low built locomotive with outside cylinders and square windows in the back of the cab was photographed in June 1901, at work on standard gauge tipping wagons at the Long Newton embankments; presumably this was one of the three narrow gauge Black Hawthorn 0-6-0 saddle tanks converted to standard gauge. As the embankments rose, the inclines to their tops, now grassy tracks, provided an exciting contrast to the flat 'main line'; locomotive driver 'Hell-fire Jack' was renowned for rushing these inclines with spectacular pyrotechnics.

Grassholme in Lunedale

Returning to the dales, John Scott's agreement with the N.E.R. for a siding was dated 15 January 1901 and the location of 'Grassholme Reservoir Siding' box (or ground frame) was 766 yards beyond Mickleton station box, where the siding key was kept. The lever frame was dated 1885 and may well have been transferred from 'Scott's Siding' after its years in use there. The connection trailed into the Barnard Castle - Middleton-in-Teesdale branch line on the left when bound for Middleton and the sidings, probably either

At 10 April 1906, the view is northward. As the bank is built up from this stage, the clay core will be packed in, founded on this concrete shoe and the concrete below it. Another 6-coupled loco by Manning Wardle is 'blowing off'.

two or three in number, diverged trailing. The widening of the cutting to accommodate these sidings can be seen from Pipely Bridge, which carries the Lunedale byroad over the N.E.R. route at this point. Scott's line left the sidings near the box, but independent of the N.E.R. line. It crossed a meadow, followed the slopes above the bank of a stream and soon attained a mainly straight and steadily climbing route up the pastures towards the present pair of waterworks houses near Grassholme dam, about one and a quarter miles from the junction. Above the left hand end of the embankment construction were the hutted workshops and offices and a locomotive shed, believed to be a long single-road structure, also men's living huts. A line continued up the valley, through the site of the bank and ran for about two miles on the bed to reach the puddlefield, the ribbed and ridged excavations of which are visible above the southern bank of the finished reservoir, approaching its head. The line went on for about a further half mile to the construction of Selset weir, installed for controlling the river Lune as it flowed towards the reservoir. The end of the line was thus about four miles from the N.E.R. junction. As mentioned, Scott started his line in January 1901. It involved a fair amount of earthworks and took several months to build. By the end of 1901 the puddle trench for the embankment was being excavated. The year 1903 witnessed setbacks. In February the consultant, Mr Mansergh, reported the need to go down to 60ft below the intended depth for the trench at its south end. In early October of that year torrential rain caused dramatic flooding at the site and a photograph shows the lower level tracks submerged, undermined and, in parts, washed away. However, also that month, it was reported that the concrete filling of the bottom of the trench was well in hand as was another major part of the works, a connecting tunnel about two miles long from near the top end of Grassholme reservoir to Hury in Baldersdale. After that, the work seems, from accounts and photographs, to have gone forward steadily but nevertheless completion was not until September 1914;

In sight of completion, looking northerly, we see 'pitching' of the main embankment at Grassholme on 31 August 1911. Loco GRASSHOLME and bywash bridge visible.

the junction with the N.E.R. disappeared from that Company's records in a supplement dated 1 January 1915. The project had occupied 14 years and the resultant dam of 300 yards length held back a lake one and three quarter miles long and containing 1333 million gallons of water, about the capacity of Hury and Blackton combined. The water is about 900ft above sea level. Subsequently, in 1955-60, Selset reservoir of 2900 million gallons capacity behind a dam of 1000 yards long has been built by Balfour Beatty & Co. Ltd - just upstream of Selset weir.

The heaviest traffics on the Grassholme railway were clay down the valley from puddlefield to embankment and stone, brought from Catcastle quarry, Lartington; this came over the N.E.R., who in those days ran morning and afternoon goods trains daily on the Middleton branch, and was placed in the exchange sidings, from which Scott brought the wagons up his line to the site. His trains were sometimes hauled and sometimes propelled. There was also work on the Lunedale-Baldersdale tunnel and it is said that Scott's locomotives zig-zagged up the hillside to reach the No.1 and No.2 shafts; there was (also?) rope-hauled narrow gauge working in connection with the No.2 shaft.

All the locomotives on the main duties were six-coupled saddle tanks by Manning Wardle, having inside cylinders of 12in x 17in or 12in x 18in. Six are listed. Of these, GRASSHOLME (1901) and DANBY LODGE (1903) were delivered to Grassholme and recalled on that job. DERWENTHAUGH (1896) came from a Tyne valley job of Scott, has been recalled in Lunedale and figures in a picture of Grassholme dam in 1907. TEES VALLEY has been remembered here and would come from Long Newton after completion there. DARLINGTON, photographed near Grassholme dam trench as early as 1902 had been secured second-hand. It thus seems that five Mannings were here at one time or another. Their livery was green, with gold lining, immaculate. They were well maintained notwithstanding fairly common derailments - soon put right with the aid of ramps, ropes and another locomotive for pulling.

Three Manning Wardle 12-inch six-coupled locomotives were advertised for auction at a sale of 18 August 1914 at Lartington quarry and Grassholme 'on completion of contract for Tees Valley Water Board'. These would presumably be three from among DANBY LODGE, DARLINGTON, DERWENTHAUGH, GRASSHOLME and TEES VALLEY.

A steam roller was prominent in views of the Grassholme bank from April 1906 onwards; with its front roller and pair of wide roller-wheels at the rear, it could be the Aveling from Baldersdale but if so it had been modified meanwhile by fitting of a canopy to give a little protection to engine and driver. Wagons used included Scott's tip wagons but N.E.R. vehicles also worked on the site tracks.

J.M.Price Williams was resident engineer for Mansergh & Sons. J.A.McLellan was in charge at site for John Scott, the contractor.

A study of June 1970 captures the surviving contract office of 1901, timber on stone base - looking up the slope to the road, the dam is away right of Arthur Chambers, he being engaged on fieldwork-cartography.

Locomotives, all standard gauge, of John Scott at Long Newton and Grassholme

    These locomotives have been mentioned but are set out more fully below; all will be seen to be by Manning Wardle, of Leeds, and all but one coming new to John Scott at one or another of his sites of work.

DARLINGTON	0-6-0 Saddle tank ic 12in x 18in
	by Manning Wardle 1309 of 1895 - new 10/9/1895 to J. Wilson Son, Heaton Lodge Siding, with their name MIRFIELD (after nearby town and station); the firm shared in the building for the L & N W R of the new 'Spen Valley line', which opened from 1/10/1900. The loco became DARLINGTON of John Scott, apparently first at Middlesbrough, and it was illustrated at Grassholme in 4/1902.
	After the Grassholme era, the engine passed to Shanks & McEwan, Scots contractors, and figured at the new works for William Beardmore & Co. Ltd on the old-established site at Mossend iron and steelworks; W.B.'s production there ceased in 1921 but S & McE locos (and some of W.B.) lay around for years - until Colvilles took over the site in 1934 and proceeded to build themselves from about 1936. DARLINGTON worked for S & McE on their part of the Edinburgh and Glasgow new road project of 1925-34.
DERWENTHAUGH	0-6-0 Saddle tank ic 12in x 17in
	by Manning Wardle 1313 of 1896 - new 17/6/1896 to John Scott at Derwenthaugh on Tyne.
	Illustrated at Grassholme in 10/1907.
	The makers attribute the loco to William Beardmore & Co. Ltd, at Parkhead Forge, Glasgow, maybe by circa 1914-15, although it would not be suitable for the classic Forge, so probably was used in developments at Mossend or elsewhere, in wartime. Later in the first world war, believed at Ministry of Munitions (MM), Cardonald, on Clydeside. It was also used by F.D. Huntingdon Ltd on factory building at Ellesmere Port.
GRASSHOLME	0-6-0 Saddle tank ic 12in x 18in
	by Manning Wardle 1513 of 1901 - new 2/9/1901 to John Scott at Mickleton, as GRASSHOLME.
	After the Grassholme job finished c1914, it probably had a 'wartime' career and was advertised by the M.M., at Crewe, 21/5/1919. Ownership by Thomas Summerson & Sons Ltd of Albert Hill Foundry, Darlington, probably followed (confirmed by the makers, but without dates), probably finally in copper at Landore (but not Lancashire).
TEES VALLEY	0-6-0 Saddle tank ic 12in x 18in
	by Manning Wardle 1594 of 1903 - new 25/2/1903 to John Scott at Goosepool for Long Newton and believed to have moved to Grassholme territory.
	Later : with Charles Baker & Sons, contractors of Chesterfield (and Doncaster), nominally at Gresford but in fact engaged in construction of the Great Central Railway branch off their Wrexham, Mold & Connahs Quay line, to the site of the proposed Llay Main colliery; the railway construction began circa 5/1914. The loco appears to have stayed at the colliery site for some years, maybe covering shunting required until the colliery was commissioned, specifically during 1921-23 when drawing of coal commenced. Under an order of 23/11/1921 in the books of Markham & Co. Ltd, of Chesterfield, repairs were carried out but it is not clear to the writer whether done at Llay Main or Chesterfield; Manning Wardle recorded Markhams' name, probably when supplying spares for this work. Markhams also figured prominently in the promotion and early ownership of Llay Main colliery and, as heavy engineers, they supplied and installed winding engines and other plant.
DANBY LODGE	0-6-0 Saddle tank ic 12in x 18in
	by Manning Wardle 1595 of 1903 - new 6/3/1903 to John Scott as DANBY LODGE (after the family residence) at Grassholme Sidings for the Grassholme project.
	This loco, like TEES VALLEY above, was with Charles Baker & Sons on construction of the G.C.R. Llay Main branch line. In 1/1916, Charles Baker advertised it at Chesterfield 'on completion of a contract' (probably the foregoing job) and they sold it that month. The Ministry of Munitions (MM) advertised it lying at the Filling Factory, Chilwell (near

MIDDLESBROUGH, with inside cylinders 12in x 18in, built 1903 by Manning Wardle of Leeds and seen before delivery to Mr John Scott at his Goosepool site on lower Teesside for the Long Newton job.

Nottingham) in 6/1919. In its perambulations (as jotted into Manning Wardle's books), Gresford figured (presumably truly Llay Main) and Horbury also appeared. Around 1930, the loco was engaged in the diversion of the L.M.S. Railway's Cheadle (Staffordshire) branch and it was stored there in 12/1933 - moving on by 5/1936 to L.M.S. Beeston sleeper works, and there until at least 1948.

MIDDLESBROUGH   0-6-0 Saddle tank ic 12in x 18in
by Manning Wardle 1598 of 1903 - new 18/6/1903 to John Scott at Goosepool for Long Newton; it may never have worked at Grassholme - it was not recalled as being there in 1905. It was on John Scott's Vittoria Dock contract, Birkenhead, which was secured in 6/1906 and overlapped much of the Lunedale period. It ended up at the London Brick Co., Calvert, Buckinghamshire, broken up in 1948.

By way of footnote to this account of 30 years work, it is of interest to note that Mr John 'Navvy' Scott was knighted during the Grassholme era but did not like to be addressed as 'Sir John'. In 1910, he succeeded his father, Sir Walter, becoming second baronet.

The Lunedale Whinstone Company

Our map has been extended to show the line of the Lunedale Whinstone Company from 'Lunedale Quarry Siding' box (ground frame dated 1878, with key, in section), 1 mile 77 yards beyond Mickleton. This private line ran on 2ft 6in gauge, from its discharging point beside the N.E.R. siding and it reached to Greengates quarry. Its beginnings ante-date the Scott/Water authority projects in Baldersdale and Lunedale. Three locomotives have been recalled as coming, successively, and all remaining until the demise of the system soon after the 1914-18 war - the Railway Company's siding entry being deleted from 1 January 1923. The locomotives were recalled to me by name as LOTTIE (the smallest), EBENEZER (the next one to come) and ZURIEL (the newest and biggest, most used in later days). Amplification follows.

Locomotives, all 2ft 6in gauge, of the Lunedale Whinstone Company

LOTTIE   0-4-0 Tank oc 5½in dia
by Black Hawthorn 629 - ordered 26/2/1881 by the Lunedale Whinstone Company, of 33 Mosley Street, Newcastle upon Tyne, for delivery in two months.

EBENEZER   0-4-0 inverted saddle ('wing') tank oc 8½in x 12in
by W.G. Bagnall 1002 of 1888 - ordered by G. Hodsman, Lunedale Whinstone Company, and new in 7/1888.

ZURIEL   0-4-0 Tank oc 8½in x 12in
by W.G. Bagnall 1917 of 1910 for G. Hodsman & Sons Ltd, Lunedale Whinstone Company, and delivered new.
It was supplied with an inclined boiler, doubtless to ensure the firebox remaining covered on the constant steep ascent from the 'main line' junction to the Greengates quarry.

A locomotive which had been expected was-
four-coupled tank loco cyls. 7in x 12in, for 2ft 6in gauge, height of chimney not to exceed 7ft 6in, 'with snow plough extra', by Black Hawthorn 768, ordered 13/9/1883 verbally by Mr Gill to Mr B. (being Mr Black) for delivery to Lunedale Whinstone Company of Middleton-in-Teesdale within three months.

However, this order was cancelled before delivery and the loco seemingly held by Black Hawthorn; under a fresh order dated 16 April 1885 it was supplied to Kerr, Stuart & Company (postal address, London), relatively minor modifications were made, ostensible makers' plates
'Kerr Stuart & Co., London and Glasgow'
were fitted, then it was crated and consigned abroad. BH 768 as modified and 'disguised' seems (with reserve) to be one of three 2ft 6in gauge 0-4-0 tank locos supplied more or less together to India, in 1885 : research of Mr H.C. Hughes shows two of them to the Morvi Railway and one to the North Western Railway (for Military lines).

The remains of the signal box, loading bank, rustic loco shed nearby and at the top of the meadow, the narrow gauge tunnel under the Middleton-Brough road B6276 at grid reference NY954242 could still be seen in 1970. The steep but well-engineered route of about two miles to Greengates, with superb views in good weather, is a pleasure to traverse on foot and must have been a thrill to tackle aboard LOTTIE. There was also a three-eighths mile branch from close to the locomotive shed, leading into Spring Top quarry. Another, probably older, formation appeared to descend from the vicinity of Greengates quarry to the Brough road near the cottages at Bowbank and a decidedly tentative thought was that in the quarry's early days stone might have been brought down it and then conveyed by horse and cart.

The Lunedale Whinstone Company's 2ft 6in gauge railway operated circa 1882-1922 and Lunedale Quarry Siding came off the N.E.R. Middleton-in-Teesdale branch (lifted in this May 1967 view) just to the right of the photographer. The narrow gauge locomotive shed has clearly been built (right hand end) for tiny LOTTIE of 1881 and extended progressively for additions of 1888 and 1910.

Quarries 'just round the corner' above Middleton-in-Teesdale

Also sketched in on the map is Ord & Maddison's standard gauge quarry line, extending from near the station yard at Middleton-in-Teesdale for about two miles along the slopes on the south side of Teesdale. It was dismantled by Arnott Young & Company in the summer of 1952 and the two surviving locomotives were broken up in 1952-53.

They were N.E.R- 0-4-0 side tanks with inside cylinders, class 'H' (LNER Y7) -

'898' built Gateshead 1888 and acquired from the LNER in 1929

'1302' built Gateshead 1891 and acquired from the LNER in 1930

On the occasion of my first visit to see these two attractive little engines, in April 1936, there was also present -

0-4-0 Saddle tank with outside cylinders and carrying a plate

'T.D. Ridley & Son, Middlesbrough',

who was at that time a well-known loco-bodger and repairer, quite capable of disguising origins.

Higher still up Teesdale, beyond High Force and Langdon Beck the London Lead Mining Company had narrow gauge lines but these are outside the range of this account - and investigation could bring the temptation to trek on logically over the fine High Cup Nick of some 2200ft and wind down the track to Dufton, and so to Appleby-in-Westmorland.

Middleton - in - Teesdale: the village is well seen, across and northward of the Tees. The quarry line is glimpsed in close foreground. The N.E.R. engine shed looks new. Their station house and station are also in pristine condition. The drawings for the new single-storey platform buildings were dated 1888 and Mr J.F. Addyman of the North Eastern Railway Association understood the station house to be rebuilt shortly before that.

At Crossthwaite quarry, on the southern slopes of Teesdale proper, this standard gauge locomotive by Black Hawthorn is said to be the first loco here, depicted before 1914, with crew.

A wider view of Crossthwaite quarry is taken a little later than the previous one. Processing of loaded stone is apparent, so are three locos.

At the better-known Middleton quarry of Ord & Maddison, here in 1934 is the locomotive rebuilt by T.D. Ridley & Son (Ridley Shaw as one later knew them at Middlesbrough).

Ord & Maddison's 898 derived its number from its N.E.R./L.N.E.R. days, being acquired by O. & M. in 1929 and seen here in August 1952. By this time it was believed to be owned by Arnott Youngs as dismantlers of O. & M.'s plant and railways. The N.E.R./L.N.E.R. station is hidden in the trees a little below.

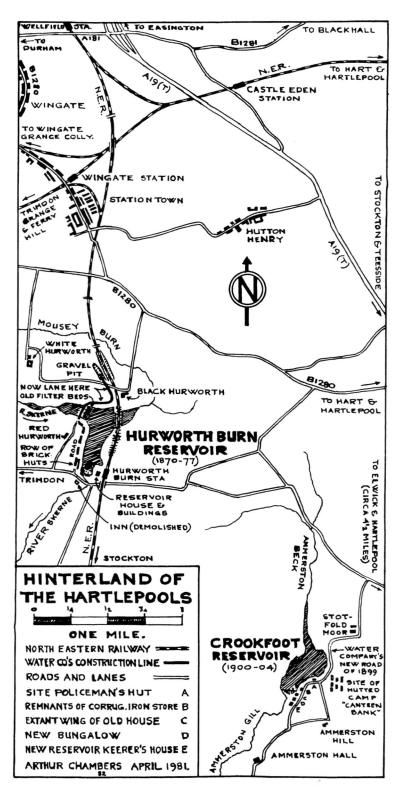

Chapter Two

Hinterland of the Hartlepools

Early days in the towns.

Whether true or false, it has long been the impression of the writer that more seagoing engineers per head of the population have emanated from the Hartlepools than from any other British mainland community, but this would be a phenomenon emerging after the middle of the nineteenth century.

The first Hartlepool dock was part of a local railway project of the eighteen-thirties. A significant advance came with the construction in 1845-47 of the dock of the Hartlepool West Harbour and Dock Company, near Stranton village; from this village developed concurrently - and during the ensuing years - the town of West Hartlepool, a centre of engineering associated especially with the needs of shipping, as well as with the importing of timber.

The Hartlepool Gas and Water Company, authorised by Act of 1846, was a product of the same period. Remarkably, the Company succeeded for a great many years in meeting the domestic demand for water from boreholes local to the town but the coming of industrial demand soon necessitated impounding reservoirs. First of these were the Hart Upper (top water level 170 ft o.d. and capacity 16½ million gallons) and Hart Lower (157ft o.d.; 5½ million gallons), sited immediately north west of the towns of Hartlepool and West Hartlepool. The consultants were Martin and Fenwick, of Leeds, who were retained in this capacity until at least the early nineteen-twenties. The contractor was George Adamson, of Leith Street, Edinburgh and construction was in 1865-66. A much larger impounding reservoir soon followed, in the pleasant and slightly upland countryside six miles inland from West Hartlepool.

Hurworth Burn.

There was an Act of 1867 and another of 1874, which latter permitted a deeper reservoir, with top water level 367ft o.d. and capacity 160 million gallons. Under the oversight of Martin and Fenwick, direct labour was employed, supplemented by labour-only subcontractors for buildings and some other specific works; notably, Johnson Carter built the reservoir house, undertook masons' work and at least some of the excavation on site.

The reservoir is fed by the river Skerne and its shape resembles a letter 'T', with the main earth embankment across the fairly narrow foot of the T. Work began in 1870 and was completed around the end of 1877. A broadly parallel development was the construction by the North Eastern Railway, under Act of 1872, of their double track secondary main line on an embankment, aligned north-south, which bounded the main portion of the reservoir on its east side. The eventual water area extended through a culvert in the N.E.R. embankment to the farther (eastern) side of that embankment. The completion of the reservoir was slightly held back awaiting progress with the N.E.R. works; the placing, by the Water Company's contractor, of protective stone pitching on part of the N.E.R. bank represented a concluding stage of the job. The railway, with station conveniently at Hurworth Burn, was opened 1 March 1880. It was closed to passengers 2 November 1931 and to all traffic from 6 July 1966. A southbound run through Hurworth Burn closed station was made on Sunday, 2 September 1956, by the Tees-Tyne Rail Tour special train of the Stephenson Locomotive Society and the Manchester Locomotive Society, originating in and returning to Manchester; locomotive was a former N.E.R. 3 cylinder 4-6-0. British Railways have run diverted passenger trains this way. For many years latterly the route was primarily one for coal traffic from Durham collieries to Teesside, conveniently keeping this traffic clear of passenger lines for almost its entire journey. This was well demonstrated when I enjoyed a run, on Friday, 24 September 1965 on the brakevan of 09.45 hrs. coal empties, South Bank Iron Works to Trimdon Grange colliery, diesel electric locomotive D6760, 30 wagons and brake. There was then no operational signal box between Redmarshall North, a junction for traffic coming in from Stockton, and Wingate South, our point of divergence for Trimdon Grange. At Hurworth Burn the N.E.R. house and associated station building were derelict and so was the railway house by the road. Return was at 11.35 hrs. from the colliery, the same locomotive now hauling 22 wagons of coal and the brake and working this load through to Cleveland (Clay Lane internal sidings of Dorman Long's steelworks). Significantly, at Wingate South we were held to await the passage, also southbound, of an ex-War Department steam 2-8-0 locomotive on 25 of coal and brake, in full cry; this would be traffic from Thornley, Hawthorn or Shotton collieries for Teesside and we followed some five minutes later through the junction, decorously, in order to allow the steam train time to pass Hurworth Burn, Wynyard and Thorpe Thewles and clear Redmarshall North.

Reverting to the reservoir at Hurworth Burn, the decision to have this deeper than at first intended, taken in 1874, led the Gas and Water Company to enquire at what price a 10 or 12 horsepower locomotive could be purchased, second-hand or new. Rails and, it is believed, six wagons were quickly ordered and in February 1875 the consultants, Martin and Fenwick, conveyed an offer from Black Hawthorn & Company, Gateshead builders of industrial locomotives, to supply a new tank locomotive with 8in diameter cylinders for £725. In the event, £875 was paid for a locomotive with 9in cylinders, namely -

HURWORTH 0-4-0 Tank cylinders 9in x 16in, to 'standard specification',
gauge not recorded by the makers or the purchasers.
It was Black Hawthorn 306 of 1875 - had been built by the makers for stock under internal order of 27/10/1874 and ordered by the Hartlepool Gas and Water Company 19/2/1875 and delivered in April 1875.

Later in 1875, a line was laid 'from the gravel pit to the filter beds at Hurworth, to obtain the materials' and £457.6.2d was spent on more rails in November 1875. The filter beds were to be at the north end and the probable site is the now flooded area where the inlet from the Skerne reaches the reservoir. It was indeed pleasing, in 1977, to find the century-old gravel pit, well grown over, on the west side of the N.E.R. alignment about one third of a mile north of the reservoir and a cutting for the private access railway located between a cultivated field and the N.E.R. cutting; crossing the lane leading to Black Hurworth farm, the course almost certainly took the route to the filter site which is now a track above the northern shore. The formation could reconcile with standard or 3ft gauge. A likelihood, but not proven, is that the line also continued southwards along the western shore to reach the site of the embankment. The private road, itself formed in 1875-76, passes this way.

Also interesting is the long range of single storey brick buildings between the west side private road and the water, close to the embankment; they are locally stated to have been 'construction huts' and some still have chimneys, while a fireplace was discernible on peering into one, in 1977. The first two 'huts' built accommodated 30 navvies and were ordered to be constructed in October 1874, with two more ordered in

Locally known as 'construction huts' at Hurworth Burn reservoir, this substantial range of buildings is seen in 1977 and could be the 'huts' of 1874-1875. The N.E.R. passed on the far side of the reservoir. There is evidence, in records and on the ground, of a site railway too.

April 1875 and three more in May 1875. A house and stables had been built earlier, under orders of 1870-71, and in 1875 the stable was enlarged and a blacksmith's shop built. The reservoir house, with its associated buildings, located close to Hurworth Burn station, has the air of a converted farmstead but the style is appropriate to 1870-75. In the days of construction, an inn, since vanished, was sited on the side of the public road, opposite to the dam.

Crookfoot.

Crookfoot reservoir is south of the road from Hurworth Burn to the Hartlepools. The turn to reach it is two miles from Hurworth Burn station and a mile-long byroad was built in 1899 to order of the Gas and Water Company in order to reach Crookfoot - much of it a decidedly rough road when writing.

The reservoir occupies a secluded site, amidst upland pastures, plantations and scattered farmsteads, ostensibly little changed since the construction workers departed, in 1904. It has a short earth bank at the southerly end. Top water level is 294ft o.d. and capacity 235 million gallons. It resulted from a report and recommendation of October 1897 by Martin & Fenwick; Mr Fenwick commented (in 1900) that Mr Mansergh, the distinguished water engineering consultant in London, called Crookfoot a baby reservoir.

The resident engineer, reporting to the consultants in Leeds, was F.W. Sutcliffe; his surviving letters to his principals are numerous and peculiarly uninformative but well filled out with complaints of the contractors' alleged shortcomings. Clerk of works was T.G. Phillips, who took up duty in February 1901 but died in November 1903. The bearded 'Black Bowran' was walking ganger. Thomas Siddle was appointed in October 1899 as caretaker and given occupation of house and garden, with free fuel. This would be Crookfoot House, of which only an outbuilding, in the redbrick 'half timbered' style of late Victorian country estates, remains, as the house proved damp and unsatisfactory due to inadequate foundations; its site is taken by a modern bungalow, with a modern house for the permanent keeper close by. The Company retained the use of a sitting room and bedroom in the old Crookfoot House for the duration of the work - no doubt for occupation by the resident engineer or the clerk of works.

A contract for the main reservoir works at Crookfoot was placed in August 1900 with W.& J. Foster, of West Hartlepool, subsequently referred to as of Bingley. The Crookfoot to West Hartlepool main was laid by contractors John Hardy and Richard Atkinson.

Clay was secured at the site, and put through a pugmill; it seemingly was employed right down to trench foundations, without concrete. Stone, some 2000 tons, was brought in from outside. Deliveries of imported materials were in general made via Hurworth Burn station, a contribution to siding costs being paid to the North Eastern Railway. The Sanderson family, farmers, residing at Ammerston* Hall, a house acquired so it is said by Lord Londonderry as far back as 1600, provided horses under contract for road haulage to the site. The Gas and Water Company's own trap met the Engineer at West Hartlepool on his visits.

Men walked daily some six miles each way from the Hartlepools but temporary huts - five initially and then two larger ones - were built for workers and sited in a rising meadow to the south east of the site and this became known as 'Canteen Bank'. The canteen was licensed. Bill Hay was canteen manager; a minute of December 1902 records that W.A. Hay had again been convicted for drunkeness. There was a resident constable, from February 1901 to March 1904, with quarters in, so it is said, part of the combined canteen, store and house. Significantly, his appointment was as game watcher for the period of the works; with Wynyard Park in proximity, Lord Londonderry's pheasants had to be protected against marauders.

In general, the work was carried on with reasonable despatch. Near completion, in April 1903, a significant slip in the embankment necessitated six months extension of time, Fosters being paid for the remedial and preventative work called for by Mr Fenwick, with whom at this time a further technical adviser, Mr Watson, collaborated, along with Mr Thomas Bower (engineer of the Company 1884-1900; engineer and general manager 1900-1914). Completion was around 31 March 1904 and formal opening

*Spelling? The Ordnance Survey have used Amerston and I have even encountered Hammerston.

was on 31 August 1904. Subsequent history included modest alterations at the bank in 1920 and 1925. An alarm on 4 March 1947, in a winter of classic severity, arose from the cracking of the masonry of the valvetower 21ft below top water level; this was due to severe frost and an ice pack averaging 9in thick on the reservoir and around the tower.

Site railway tracks have been recalled but with 'bogies' pushed by hand and my informant would not admit to horses or locomotives being employed for motive power.

W.& J.Foster, stated of Hartlepool, tendered in October 1902 to the Bury and District Joint Water Board to build reservoirs near Haslingden Grane in Lancashire. They secured the order and began work there in December 1902 and no doubt anticipated completion at Crookfoot within six months or thereabouts, after which all the firm's resources could be concentrated on the Lancashire job. But in the spring of 1903 there occurred the slip which extended the Crookfoot project and would be a cause of financial anxiety to the contractors. John Foster, of Stranton House, Foggy Furze, West Hartlepool, died in August 1903, aged sixty-nine; he had retired ten years previously from public works contracting. Mr W. Foster died in January 1904 and the firm and its management passed to his son J.L. Foster. Although Crookfoot was finished in 1904 and the firm were paid off that year, they were in trouble at Haslingden, where men were dismissed or left their service and progress was poor in 1904-05. By April 1905, Mr Sam Foster represented the firm at Haslingden but in June 1905 Fosters negotiated the transfer of their Lancashire contact to the firm of Phineas Drake & Sons, Bradford.

Several 3ft gauge steam locomotives were used by Fosters at Haslingden Grane but the only one likely to have been brought there by them was called CROOKFOOT and was said to be a 9in cylinder 'flat tank tunnel engine', thought to be in the early Kilmarnock tradition, but it was not Andrew Barclay 719 of 1892 as has been quoted elsewhere. The work with puddle clay would surely call for at least one 3ft gauge locomotive at Crookfoot in the relatively mechanised era of 1900-03 and it is a reasonable surmise that the engine CROOKFOOT, almost certainly second-hand, acquired its name at this rural location in the county of Durham.

The gas undertaking was nationalised in fairly recent years but the Hartlepools Water Company continued to administer the reservoirs which have been described, and also the areas of supply. No attempt has been made to give an account of their steam, or other, pumping plant down the years.

This is the vintage 'Scots' 3ft gauge locomotive used by contractors W & J Foster on reservoir construction at Haslingden Grane in Lancashire and known there as CROOKFOOT. It was the only one of their locos at Haslingden likely to have been brought from their job at Crookfoot for Hartlepool, in circa 1903. It was *not* Andrew Barclay 719 of 1892 but had probably been 'concocted' from machines of earlier date than that.

Chapter Three

Wearhead and Waskerley Moors

Introduction.

The county of Durham boasts magnificent moorland on its westerly flank and this is most notably penetrated by Weardale and the valley of the Rookhope burn, its principal tributary.

In the head of Weardale, the North Eastern Railway built their terminal station at Wearhead, some 1100 ft above o.d. A mile beyond is Cowshill, the last hamlet in the dale, 1200 ft o.d. Another four miles westward, the road to Alston in Cumbria crosses the Pennine watershed at Killhope Cross, a classic 2056 ft o.d. The name of this summit is associated with the Killhope burn and moor but appeared to have another connotation when I first made my way from Alston to the railhead at Wearhead, by pedal cycle, a number of years ago.

During the nineteen-thirties it was a delight to leave behind the traffic of Lancashire and Cheshire, where already the popular roads were jammed with motor cars each weekend, to travel to a station on the Settle-Carlisle line, surmount the high Pennines and finally sweep down to a dale where the motor car, held back by the severe industrial depression in north east England, was seldom seen. The quiet roads were devoid of 'improvement', the railway conveyed passengers, goods and minerals. The Rookhope, Wear and other valleys provided an archaeological feast of onetime mineral workings and associated lesser railways. A splendid guide to research in this field has since been provided : *'The Railways of Weardale'* by Tom E. Rounthwaite, R.C.T.S. 1965.

Above the small town of Stanhope were established, on the northern slopes of Weardale, the quarries and limeworks which led to the opening of the Stanhope and Tyne line in 1834. This railway, which eventually became part of the N.E.R., climbed the spectacular Crawleyside and Weatherhill inclines, crossed the moor to Waskerley, a railwaymen's village with locomotive shed and other depots at 1150 ft o.d., and descended Nanny Mayor's bank to reach Consett and its ironworks. Hisehope, Smiddy Shaw and Waskerley reservoirs were formed on this moor, with aid from the S. & T. line, Tunstall reservoir was a little to the south and Beldon was projected in Northumberland, with a railway link from the S. & T. route. Eventually, Burnhope reservoir was constructed above Wearhead, bringing an influx of little locomotives and their folk to the upper dale, along with all the other plant and people for a major civil engineering work in the age of steam.

The earlier reservoirs are shown on our map of Waskerley moor and environs and they may be summarised as follows.

Waskerley reservoir - immediately south of the S.& T. line, capacity 450 million gallons and top water level 1172 ft o.d., for the Weardale and Shildon District Waterworks Company, authorised by their Act of 1866. Tenders were obtained in 1868 and completion was in 1872. Filter beds at Waskerley were brought into use in January 1881. The supplies were mostly destined for Bishop Auckland and Shildon districts and service reservoirs were built thereabouts in 1869-71.

Tunstall reservoir - some four miles further down the valley of the Waskerley beck, capacity 520 million gallons and top water level 720 ft o.d., for the same Company, under authority of the same Act; built 1873-78 and commissioned in 1880, after a leak had been rectified. Filter beds at Tunstall were not completed until 1901.

Smiddy Shaw reservoir - immediately north of the S. & T. line, capacity 297 million gallons (alternatively 305 million gallons), top water level 1120 ft o.d., for the Consett Waterworks Company of 1860. Design was by William Bouch of Darlington (locomotive superintendent of the Stockton & Darlington section of the North Eastern Railway and not to be confused with his brother Sir Thomas Bouch, of Edinburgh, whose Tay bridge suffered disaster in 1879), with collaboration from Thomas Hawksley, notable London

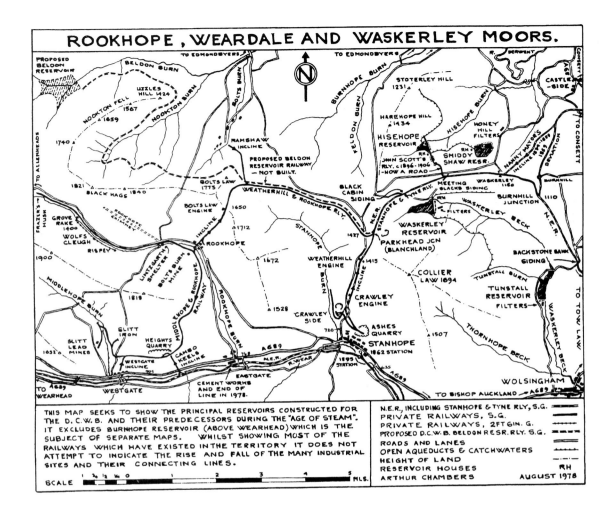

consultant in water engineering. Authority was the Consett Waterworks Act of 1869 and construction 1869-77. William Bouch died in Weymouth on 19 January 1876, much respected by the Board of the Waterworks Company, with whom he had worked over the years.

Hisehope reservoir - about a mile westward from Smiddy Shaw, capacity 106 million gallons and top water level 1127 ft o.d., for the Consett Waterworks Company, authorised by the Consett Waterworks Act of 1894 and constructed by contractor John Scott, of Newcastle. The contract was placed around September 1896; work was prolonged by trouble with the foundation cut-off trench and then by a labour shortage in 1900, completion being reported in July 1906, by which time the Weardale Water Act of 1902 had merged the Consett Waterworks Company with the Weardale and Shilton District Waterworks Company. The new body was styled the Weardale and Consett Water Company.

Honey Hill filter beds - about a half mile north east of Smiddy Shaw, completed 1897 but since supplemented and superseded by more modern plant at the site; this treats the waters of Hisehope and Smiddy Shaw and those from faraway Burnhope, insofar as the latter are destined for territory of the Durham County Water Board.

Stanhope & Tyne Railway: a good old scene at Crawleyside incline head and engine house, above Stanhope, with its staff - looking to the upper incline (Weatherhill) and the moors.

Beldon reservoir - a project of the Consett Waterwoks Company to designs of T. & C. Hawksley and the subject of parliamentary plans deposited 30 November 1901. The scheme was overtaken by the merger of 1902 and the genesis of the Burnhope scheme, which would provide a reservoir of far greater capacity than Beldon.

Service reservoirs - reference has been omitted to the service reservoirs, nearer the towns supplied by both former Companies. For the record, the Durham Water Company had been taken over by the Weardale and Shildon Company under the Weardale and Shildon District Waterworks Act of 1879.

Stockton & Darlington locomotive No.26 PILOT is masquerading as No.10 (AUCKLAND) for the S & D R celebrations of 1875. It is property of Consett Water Company and is discussed in the text, under 'Smiddy Shaw reservoir'.

After a jolly morning outing, 20 September 1961, 9.50am, No.63404 Q6 0-8-0 locomotive (N.E.R. T2 class) is coming back, propelling the goods, Weatherhill to Burnhill, and thence Consett; a fine grade of moulders' sand was one of the products of Weatherhill. The 'agent's house' at Waskerley carried Stockton & Darlington Railway plaque K/8, just concealed by the middle wagon.

The use of railways for waterworks construction on Waskerley moors.

A siding, or sidings, existed at Black Cabin, on the S. & T. line of the N.E.R., 1 mile 32 chains from Parkhead and 2 miles 18 chains from Waskerley - put in by the time of compilation of a list of sidings dated 1894. It was attributed by the N.E.R. to 'Weardale and Shildon Water Company', subsequently amended (presumably in 1902) to 'Weardale and Consett Water Company'. The location would be ideal for access to *Waskerley reservoir* and it is reasonable to surmise that the siding was first put in for the construction works (1868-72) of the Waterworks Company at *Waskerley reservoir* and retained for their occasional use, for example when the filter beds were made. It has not emerged whether a branch railway or tramway was put down on the byroad to the site of *Waskerley dam*, about three quarters of a mile, or indeed whether that byroad was itself made on a tramway formation.

Smiddy Shaw appears to have associations with constructional railways at two points in its development. An interesting locomotive links with the dates of the reservoir's construction, 1869-77. The locomotive was Stockton & Darlington Railway No.26 PIL0T, built by Kitching of Darlington in 1840. It was a 0-6-0 loco with reversed and severely inclined outside cylinders, with return flue boiler, fired from 4-wheeled tender ahead of the smokebox, also hauling a 4-wheeled truck or tender with water tank; thus it was broadly of the family familiar through the preserved S,& D.R. No.25 DERWENT of 1845 (and 1925 centenary fame). Historian Kenneth Hoole ascertained that the North Eastern Railway order for cut up of PILOT was dated 1867 and this loco was replaced in the Company's stock in 1868 and 'sold to the Consett Water Company.' Another distinguished historian, E.L. Ahrons, writing in *The Locomotive Magazine* 15 August 1925, reported that the engine was borrowed back by the N.E.R from the Waterworks Company in 1875, received in a poor state and put into order under the disguise of No.10 AUCKLAND; this pretence was designed to display a supposed product of Timothy Hackworth! He also says that, after use in the 1875 'S.& D.R.' celebrations, the number was painted out and the engine returned to the Waterworks Company. The photograph reproduced in *The Locomotive Magazine* shows the loco looking disreputable, with no name carried and No.10 painted in white on the plinth of the dome. The location is a barren spot, strewn with sleepers and bricks - with no background fence and the corner or end of a building to the right. Ken Hoole suggested to me that this site was at the N.E.R's North Road Works, Darlington, although admittedly not with the background usually adopted there. Another good friend, Bernard Roberts, suggested that the scene has all the air of a reservoir construction site on moorlands Waskerley way, e.g. at *Smiddy Shaw*: intriguing, and bear in mind that William Bouch put in much civil and mechanical work for the S.& D.R. and was engineer for the *Smiddy Shaw* reservoir.

Independently, recollections have been passed down of a railway at *Smiddy Shaw* and this would be in the early nineteen-twenties. There was an agreement between the L N E Railway and Balfour, Beatty & Co. Ltd, contractors specialising in tunnelling works, dated 31 December 1921 for a tramway 'between Stanhope and Waskerley' (meaning leaving the S.& T. line somewhere between Stanhope kilns and Waskerley). The agreement was terminated 13 May 1923. It is significant that the private access road south of the reservoir and running westward to the tunnel mouth is slightly elevated by banking and well aligned; probably a line was made here to help in making the tunnel, through which the raw water from Burnhope to Honey Hill filters can pass. Water was obtained in the Burnhope valley in the earlier 'twenties and an associated aqueduct commissioned, bound initially for *Waskerley reservoir*. The tunnel portal near *Smiddy Shaw* is dated 1926 and bears the initials of the Durham County Water Board. When Burnhope reservoir, above Wearhead, was completed in the 'thirties, the volume of water passing from the upper dale was vastly increased.

John Scott as contractor employed a standard gauge railway between the S. & T.(N.E.R.) line and *Hisehope reservoir* site, in the 1890's. The N.E.R. connection was obviously at Meeting Slack (alternatively styled Meeting Slacks), 2 miles 21 chains from Parkhead and 1 mile 29 chains from Waskerley, where the Railway Company show a siding in their 1894 list; it was entered as 'Consett Iron Company' (and thus may date from before *Hisehope* secured its Act of 1894), but the entry was altered in manuscript to 'Weardale and Consett Water Company'. The widening of the N.E.R. formation at Meeting Slack is apparent, also the probable alignment over the adjacent moor to the main road - a modest cart road in the 'nineties - which would be crossed on the level. The access road thence to the reservoir displays all the indications of a railway alignment - first on slight embankment, then descending at about 1 in 20 on reverse curves in cutting, finally on a substantial embankment for the straight descent to near the caretaker's house and the south end of the dam. The N.E.R. siding list was endorsed 'Only occasionally used by the Weardale & Consett Water Company for delivery of pipes to their waterworks'. This however was probably noted in later years when Scott's railway had vanished but the siding facility was retained for occasional supplies; it was in fact a loop 143 yards long, with trap points at each end.

On the ground, it has appeared to me that Scott may have had railways or tramways also on the north side of the site for making the stone lined feeder channel and for bringing masonry to the main embankment, which is faced on its water side with substantial stone pitching blocks. Hisehope Head quarry, about three quarters of a mile north west of the site, could be a source, although I have failed to trace a connecting line.

Remembering that Scott's contract was dated September 1896, that there were site problems in 1900 and completion about mid 1906, it is most interesting to read a retrospective autobiographical account, probably written 'from memory', by Jeremiah Simpson. He states with date 1901 (maybe an approximation) that he sublet his quarries at Storeton and went to *Hisehope* as walking ganger for Sir John Scott, contractor. He quotes the engineers as C. & J. Hawksley, of Westminster, and the contract value as £175,000 He gives the puddle trench as 1800ft long, 10ft wide and 80ft deep, with concrete walls 24in thick on each side (interesting !) and 6ft puddle-clay core.

Mr Simpson's account goes on to mention a bywash and catchwaters (note my stone-lined feeder drain) and heavy masonry (according with my observations), and 'large quarries on the works'. 'Puddle fields and clay mills 4½ miles away' represent further intelligence and provide good reason for powerful railway locomotives.

Also mentioned are six steam cranes, one steam navvy and four locomotives.

My suggested list of locomotives follows:

Locomotives, standard gauge, of John Scott - on Hisehope reservoir construction.

WASKERLEY 0-6-0 Saddle tank ic 12in x 17in
by Manning Wardle 1312 of 1895; ordered by Scott 7/9/1895; tried in steam 26/2/1896; sent away by MW 2/11/1896 to John Scott at Waskerley, implicitly for use on the Hisehope run and site lines. The final delay is strange but note that John Scott secured the Hisehope contract circa 8/1896. This loco was recalled to me as employed by Monk & Newell on their construction works for the Cardiff Railway Company, which would be somewhere between 5/1898 and 8/1906; maybe Scott hired it for a time to M & N.
The loco followed up by working for John Scott on his job constructing the New Vittoria Dock, Birkenhead, contract secured June 1906, plant sold up about 3 /1914.
Its subsequent history was in other hands.

DERWENTHAUGH 0-6-0 Saddle tank ic 12in x 17in
by Manning Wardle 1313 of 1896
which had been new to Scott at Derwenthaugh on Tyne and was at Grassholme by 10/1907.
This was the only one of the Manning Wardle locomotives mentioned when describing the Scott contracts for the Tees Valley Water Board at Long Newton and Grassholme, 1901-14, which is believed to have put in a spell at Hisehope.

WILLIAM BLACK 0-6-0 Saddle tank ic 12in x 18in
by Black Hawthorn of Gateshead 1115 of 1896 - ordered 17/5/1895 by *William* Scott possibly for the contractor's work on Consett Iron Company developments in the hinterland of Derwenthaugh but effectively for the Hisehope job. Repaired by Manning Wardle of Leeds in 1905, presumably on completion of its time at Hisehope. It was on Scott's Birkenhead dock job, believed throughout 1906-14; they then parted with it to a long and complex career down to 1930.

TYNESIDER 0-6-0 Saddle tank ic 12in x 18in
by Black Hawthorn 1116 of 1896 - ordered similarly along with the preceding loco and likewise thought to reach Hisehope early in its life and remain until repairs by Manning Wardle in 1905 and ensuing work for Scott through seemingly the whole duration of his Birkenhead job. Disposal 1914 and an involved history with other owners down to breaking up at Birkenhead in 1951 (In our days it carried no 'BH' plates).

No hint has been traced of direct access to *Tunstall reservoir*, of which construction started in 1873, with commissioning achieved in 1880. However, for many years there was a siding connection on the North Eastern Railway line 1 mile 47 chains south of Burnhill Junction and 3 miles 46 chains north of Tow Law. In the 1892 appendix to working timetables and the 1895 list of sidings, it was titled 'Baxton Bank Siding.' In 1895 it was attributed to the Weardale and Shildon Water Company, also being used by one J. Bates, a stone merchant. He was in time succeeded by Thomas Bates, whose name was finally deleted in a Railway Company circular of 1 November 1919. By an agreement with the N.E.R. dated 7 September 1908, another stone merchant, W. Hellawell, gained a share in the use of the siding. The title had changed to 'Backstone Bank Depots and Siding' (note spelling) and that of the water authority to Weardale and Consett Water Company. The siding remained listed, with ground frame, until the line between Burnhill Junction and the outskirts of Crook ceased to be used. This line closed to passengers 1 May 1939, to goods 4 March 1940, was used for storage of rolling stock and was lifted in 1953-54. Presumably the water authority retained at least a nominal interest. The siding was on the western side of the line, with access at its northerly end and a clear standage length of 127 yards, evidently inside catch points. It was about a half mile from the head of *Tunstall reservoir* and rather over 300 feet above top water, with a connecting lane which could be used by horse-hauled vehicles. Inspection of the site (in 1979) revealed sleeper marks of a single siding road and the dividing stone walls of three coal cells, also the remains of a probable warehouse; stone sleepers were incorporated into the cells and warehouse as copings. It is confirmed that coal for the Water Company houses at Tunstall was delivered to the siding by rail and fetched by cart.

Beldon in more detail

The Beldon scheme, if proceeded with, would have involved a railway of 11 miles 3 furlongs in length over a moorland route varying from about 1500ft to 1700ft and gradually falling to 1350ft at the site of the dam in Northumberland. Vistas would have been superb. The parliamentary plans described a 'tramroad from the south east end of the embankment of Beldon reservoir to north of the junction of the Weatherhill & Rookhope Railway and Stanhope & Waskerley mineral branch of the North Eastern Railway. This last is the S. & T. line and the W. & R. Railway was the private line of the Weardale Iron Company from Parkhead to Bolts Law stationary engine and thence down to Rookhope village. Mr Tom Rounthwaite, in writing of that railway, mentions a passenger train service for ironstone miners, using two old railway carriages and a steam locomotive of the Iron Company.

The relevant parliamentary plan shows the Beldon waterworks railway from a proposed junction with the N.E.R. at Parkhead, immediately north of the Iron Company's junction, taking a parallel but independent course until its divergence away north west from the Iron Company's line. Westbound, the ruling grade was to be 1 in 56 but the intended descent to the site was as steep as 1 in 30, 1 in 35 and 1 in 40 in parts.

The Weardale Iron Company's railway between Parkhead and Rookhope was officially closed in March 1923 but in fact survived for many more years, certainly until the second world war. It is worth digressing to quote from *'The Chloride Chronicle'* dated Christmas 1929, the house journal of Chloride Electrical Storage Company Limited, of Clifton Junction, Manchester (now Chloride Group Limited). The account reads -

'Electric traction on a grouse moor

Few stretches of country offer better shooting than is to be had over the wild moorlands of Durham, and these great natural advantages are greatly enhanced when a railway is found abandoned on the grouse moor - always provided, of course, that one knows what to do with a railway when found.

Mr A.E. Bainbridge, of Stanhope Castle, Co. Durham, has shown the utmost resource with his railway. During the grouse shooting season it had been customary to use ponies to assist the guns in getting about, but in 1924 the Weardale Steel Company abandoned a single rail track of standard gauge called the Rookhope and Millop (sic) line, which runs from Parkhead station for about 4½ miles across wild but fairly level moorland to Bolt's Law Terminus. Mr Bainbridge, who owned the shooting rights, took over the track and decided to use an electric locomotive instead of the ponies.

A suitable truck being obtained, it was fitted with a 50-volt motor of 6 h.p., the drive being direct through reduction gear, and a series parallel controller was fitted centrally. The truck was then equipped with two Exide-Ironclad batteries, type IMV3, each having 24 cells. It was arranged that each battery should work independently, and for this purpose a change-over switch was fitted. The batteries are underslung on the chassis and propel the truck at a speed of approximately ten miles an hour.

From August to December each year this electric truck is used for conveying shooting parties to various points, three trips a day being the average, or a total daily journey of about 26 miles; whilst from December to August it is in use fairly regularly for stores and miscellaneous haulage.

When the batteries require recharging they are taken by motor lorry to the Castle, where an 11 h.p. Crossley engine driving a 3 k.w. generator supplies the current. Mr Bainbridge informs us that the batteries have given every satisfaction during their six years' service, and are still in excellent condition.

All self-respecting railways must have regulations, of course, and Mr Bainbridge's railway is no exception. Tickets are solemnly issued to passengers, complete with 'By Orders' and advertisements which make most amusing reading.'

The Chloride Chronicle.

ELECTRIC TRACTION ON A GROUSE MOOR

Few stretches of country offer better shooting than is to be had over the wild moorlands of Durham, and these great natural advantages are considerably enhanced when a railway is found abandoned on the grouse moor—always provided, of course, that one knows what to do with a railway when found.

The Electric Truck at Stanhope Castle, Co. Durham

Mr. A. E. Bainbridge, of Stanhope Castle, Co. Durham, has shown the utmost resource with his railway. During the grouse shooting season it had been customary to use ponies to assist the guns in getting about, but in 1924 the Weardale Steel Company abandoned a single line rail track of standard gauge called the Rookhope and Millop line, which runs from Parkhead station for about 4½ miles across wild but fairly level moorland to Bolt's Law Terminus. Mr. Bainbridge, who owned the shooting rights, took over the track and decided to use an electric locomotive instead of the ponies.

A suitable truck being obtained, it was fitted with a 50-volt motor of 6 h.p., the drive being direct through reduction gear, and a series parallel controller was fitted centrally. The truck was then equipped with two *Exide-Ironclad* batteries, type IMV3, each having 24 cells. It was arranged that each battery should work independently, and for this purpose a change-over switch was fitted. The batteries are underslung on the chassis and propel the truck at a speed of approximately ten miles an hour.

From August to December each year this electric truck is used for conveying shooting parties to various points, three trips a day being the average, or a total daily journey of about 26 miles; whilst from December to August it is in use fairly regularly for stores and miscellaneous haulage.

When the batteries require recharging they are taken by motor lorry to the Castle, where an 11 h.p. Crossley engine driving a 3 k.w. generator supplies the current. Mr. Bainbridge informs us that the batteries have given every satisfaction during their six years' service, and are still in excellent condition.

All self-respecting railways must have regulations, of course, and Mr. Bainbridge's railway is no exception. Tickets are solemnly issued to passengers, complete with "By Orders" and advertisements which make most amusing reading.

No. 5940	No. 7628
STANHOPE, ROOKHOPE and DISTRICT RAILWAY	**STANHOPE, ROOKHOPE and DISTRICT RAILWAY**
Weather Hill Terminus	**DOG TICKET**
Whiteley Rigg	
Meadow's Wall	Available up to FIFTY MILES travelling with Owner and at Owner's risk.
Bell's Hill	
Bolt's Law Terminus	
NOTICE	**NOTICE**
The company will not be responsible for loss of temper, looks or appetite whilst on the Company's Property. All Guns and Flasks must be unloaded. Gentlemen must provide their own Cartridges and Ladies their own powder. By Order	Dogs desiring to fight should walk. No seats guaranteed. Dogs should not bite the Conductor nor leave the car when in motion. Please do not chew the game till it is cooked. By Order

LADIES WITH PEGAMOID COMPLEXIONS SHOULD USE SMOKELESS POWDER NOT AFFECTED BY WIND OR RAIN

Reverse side of Passenger Ticket

DO YOU SUFFER FROM FLEAS, MUSCULAR RHEUMATISM, BAD TEMPER OR ANIMAL MAGNETISM? TRY FLOGGING
Col. DAMMU *writes*: "I learnt about 'FLOGGING' from my dog and tried it on my wife, since when she has never bitten me again."

Reverse side of Dog Ticket

* * *

COMPLICATED.

An Irish Officer: "Men, ye are on the ave of battle. Will yez fight or will yez run?"

"We will," shouted the men eagerly.

"Which will yez do?" says he.

"We will not," says they.

"Thank ye, me men," says he, "I thought ye would."

This page from 'The Chloride Chronicle' of Christmas 1929 associates with 'Electric traction on a grouse moor'.

The Burnhope Project

Early days and railway plans.

The waters of the Killhope and Burnhope burns combine to form the river Wear. On the northern bank above their confluence is sited the village of Wearhead and on the south bank of the Wear the railway station, opened by the North Eastern Railway, 21 October 1895, and closed to passengers from 29 June 1953, to all traffic 2 January 1961.

As far back as 1902, the Weardale Water Act, which created the Weardale and Consett Water Company, also authorised the forming of a large reservoir by construction of a massive dam on the Burnhope stream. Negotiations were opened between the old Weardale & Shildon Waterworks Company and the N.E.R. and an agreement concluded 12 May 1902 concerning *'two tramways at Wearhead station'*; it is not known why *two* tramways were necessary but doubtless the main object was to achieve a rail link from the station to the site of the proposed dam. Notwithstanding that the alternative major water scheme at Beldon and its proposed construction railway were shelved indefinitely, the powers for the Burnhope project were allowed to lapse and work not proceeded with. Their revival was inopportunely timed, plans by T. & C. Hawksley being deposited 30 November 1914 for the parliamentary session 1915. These included a 'tramway' from south of Wearhead station to the embankment site at Burnhope. The route, derived from the parliamentary plan of 1914, is shown on our map. It was to be level for 1 furlong 3 chains from the station yard, followed by 5 chains at 1 in 28 up to reach the level crossing over the main valley road, then again on a gradient of 1 in 28 for another mile (approximately) to attain the embankment top. Walking the route in 1977 (and also viewing it from across the valley), prior to locating the parliamentary plan, it seemed probable that the line would have passed *close* below the house at Low Rigg and just *above* that at Middle Rigg. The plan points to a course rather lower on the valley slopes.

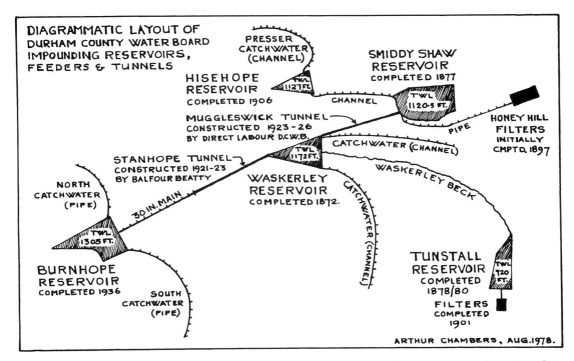

This is a diagrammatic water map, *not* showing railways, to place the Burnhope reservoir project of twentieth century in perspective with the earlier works on and about Waskerley moors.

The Weardale & Consett Water Company concluded an agreement with the N.E.R. on 2 July 1915 relative to the tramroad at Wearhead and they also agreed on other features, these latter probably concerning the course of the planned aqueducts where crossing or otherwise affecting railways. Powers were granted in 1915 but war conditions led to compulsory postponement of all the works.

Formation of the Durham County Water Board - more plans.

Rethinking after the war, the involvement of the Durham County Council and the representations of the Sunderland and South Shields Water Company led to two major connected developments. First, by Act of 1920, the Durham County Water Board was established, taking over from 31 December 1920 the rights and obligations of the Weardale & Consett Water Company, including those of 1915. Then followed the Durham County Water Board Act 1922, which provided for a higher embankment at Burnhope reservoir, an enlarged catchment area, with conduits and catchwaters (described as 'piped'), and sharing of the impounded waters 46 per cent to D.C.W.B. and 54 per cent to S. & S.S.W. Company. In its revised and final form the top water level is 1305 ft o.d. and the capacity 1357 million gallons, contained by an earth embankment 1770 ft long, 131 ft above the bed of the stream, 1312 ft o.d. on top, with the diverted road across it. The length of the reservoir is 2200 yards.

The 1922 Act provided for the 'tramway', Wearhead to Burnhope. However, the major works at Burnhope were still not put in hand. An intermediate step (under authority of the 1915 Act) was the construction by D.C.W.B. of an intake and weir on the Burnhope stream about 500 yards up-valley from the site for the dam and a 30in diameter pipe down the centre of the valley to enable the water to be carried to the existing plant much further east in the vicinity of the Waskerley moors. It was contemporary with this development that the permanent tunnel works (mentioned earlier) of the 1920s on the Waskerley moors were undertaken by D.C.W.B., en route to Honey Hill filters. It should be added that the first stage in these tunnel and aqueduct works was designed to deliver Burnhope waters to Waskerley reservoir, the alternative direct route to Honey Hill being constructed as a subsequent stage.

Provision was made for a siding connection at Wearhead goods yard by agreement dated 19 January 1926 between D.C.W.B. and the L.N.E.R. The Railway Company noted that the new siding connection east of Wearhead signal box was brought into use 5 March 1928 for the D.C.W.B. The parliamentary plan of 1915 suggests that the location of the Water Board sidings was to be west of the signal box and south of the Railway's coal cells. By 1926 the firm of Bradleys Ltd had a siding in this part of the L.N.E.R. goods yard and hence the two eventual sidings put in for D.C.W.B. were east of the signal box: see our map. A long holding siding for Water Board traffic was added in 1930 on the extreme north of the Wearhead station area between the run-round loop and the river Wear.

Wearhead station is behind the camera and Wearhead village to the right over the Wear bridge, the main road A689 being in immediate foreground; the newly-made access road of the Durham County Water Board is ahead. The two massive L.N.E.R. railway carriages, off their bogies, are installed as dwellings, including a barber's shop. The Ford car registration UP4408 has been provided by the DCWB for Stanley S. Allderidge, their resident engineer.

Robert Bradley and brother Hartley Bradley had set up a tarmacadam plant here and they had other interests in the dale over a period. To the knowledge of John Dawson, son of the onetime station master at Eastgate, Bradleys had three Sentinel road steam wagons which in the 1920s hauled loads of pipes for cut-and-cover work (presumably on the aqueduct earlier mentioned) from Eastgate station up the dale side and away over the Rookhope burn. They had come from steam haulage in Lancashire. Fluorspar exploitation at Ireshopeburn also ensued. Eventually (1930's) at least five Sentinels were based at their depot in upper Weardale.

Two long railway carriages, then devoid of bogies, by 1930 provided dwellings (one being a barber's shop) beside the entry to the new road to Burnhope site. These were East Coast Joint Stock bow-ended clerestory vehicles of circa 1898 and probably built at York. John Dawson recalls seeing them, believed painted in red oxide, at Stanhope goods yard en route up the branch line. This was about 1926 when he was 'commuting' daily between Eastgate and school in Wolsingham.

Final project, 1930

When eventually, inspired by the County Council's urge to relieve chronic unemployment, the reservoir works went forward in 1930, it was decided to use the Board's railway sidings but to construct a road to the site in place of a railway. This was done and the private road remains in use today; the waterworks were carried on under the 1922 powers but with 'tramroad' altered to 'an access road' (on a more direct course). An Act of 1934 provided for extension of time to 4 August 1938.

The designs for the 1930 project were by Walter S. Nicholson (who was still actively concerned five years later, when he suffered an accident in course of an inspection at Burnhope), representing T. & C. Hawksley, and W.J.E. Binnie of Binnie, Deacon and Gourley; Mr Nicholson and Mr Binnie figured as joint Engineers for design and supervision. Furthermore, Edward Sandeman, consultant Engineer to the Sunderland and South Shields Water Company, participated in some degree in course of the works. This was the time of deepest industrial depression in north east England and Government grants were forthcoming. The Unemployment Grants Committee were much involved in the selection of labour. They required that the work should go to married men from the County of Durham who had been unemployed for between two and four years and that 75 per cent should be ex-service men, meaning that they had been in the armed services. Owing to demands from the Grants Committee that the work should be shared, it was a common practice for a gang to be formed and see through a particular job but then to be dismissed and another gang of men recruited for the next job. Notwithstanding all this, also the high proportion of wet and windy days and January-February spells of frost and snow, the men soon became acclimatised and put in good work. These short term workers were brought up daily in buses from Bishop Auckland and other centres.

Stanley S. Allderidge was appointed resident engineer from 13 March 1930 for the duration of the job. He came from the Silent Valley reservoir scheme of the Belfast Water Commissioners, its site being in the Mourne mountains, and brought various men with him, skilled tradesmen. Leonard Hunter Brown was assistant resident engineer. Messrs. Chrimes, Clark and Hetherington were appointed junior engineers. The walking ganger was Dai Hood, a Welshman and reputedly a 'character', who had latterly been in the Silent Valley. Also keenly interested in the works was Henry Robinson, who had been assistant engineer and (from 1918) engineer and manager of the Weardale and Consett Water Company and transferred to the D.C.W.B. on its formation, as engineer and manager.

'The construction of Burnhope reservoir' down to mid 1935 is the subject of a thoroughgoing account by S.S. Allderidge, the resident engineer, published by the Institution of Water Engineers, whose summer meeting in June 1935 included a visit to site. Whilst not going into as much technical detail as did Mr Allderidge, his account has been drawn upon freely in course of the ensuing story.

Activity commenced nominally on 6 January 1930. The building of the road from Wearhead to the site, about one mile, was begun, and completed during that year. Electric power was brought up the valley, the 'national grid' overhead transmission lines being extended 15 miles by August 1930; the Water Board

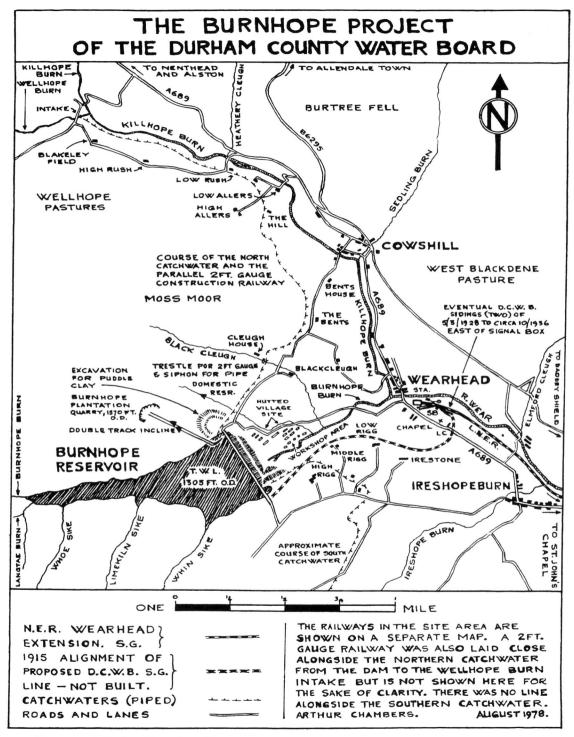

Note especially the railway from Wearhead station to Burnhope dam, authorised by Act of 1922 and indicated ---------- on our map but not constructed.

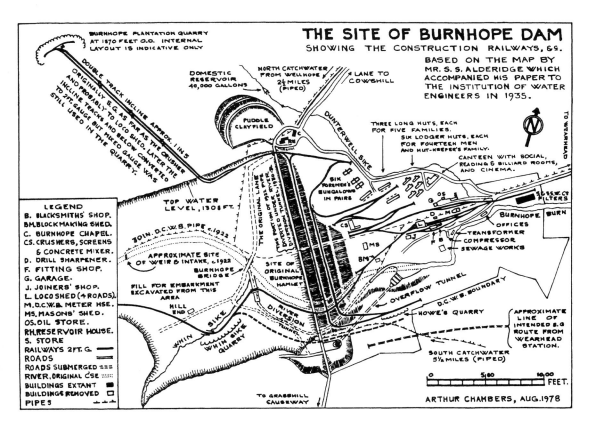

built a transformer house for stepping down the voltage. The first sods were cut on 18 July 1930 by Councillor Peter Lee, J.P., chairman of the D.C.W.B. since 1920, and Robert H. Gaymer, chairman of the S. & S.S.W. Company.

The workshops, sheds and village at Burnhope.

Workshops and stores were largely built during 1930. There was a compressor house, a fitting shop and adjoining blacksmith's shop, the latter under the charge of a smith who was also a competent welder; these shops could undertake some mechanical construction work and most maintenance and at the peak of the job were open night and day. A prudently isolated joiner's shop was built, a main stores, a separate oil stores, garage, cement shed, mason's shed and the site office. There was a locomotive shed, designed to accommodate both standard gauge and 2 ft gauge steam locomotives and having a total of four roads. There were never more than two standard gauge locomotives; one of these is believed to have arrived in 1930 and the other soon afterwards, both disposed of circa 1933, by which time standard gauge operation was superseded apart possibly from some use in the main quarry. The narrow gauge of 2ft was the same as at Trentabank (Macclesfield). Locomotives for it were acquired during 1931-33, or thereabouts, as the scale of work increased; they became numerous and monopolised the locomotive shed.

Living quarters were built for the tradesmen, during 1930-31. These were hutted houses, erected on the slopes immediately below the new access road, as it climbed the northern valley side to reach the top level of the eventual dam. Farthest up the hill were the three pairs of bungalows for six foremen and their families. Then a little lower, came the three long huts each containing five living units for families, a total of fifteen such units. Lower down the road was the group of six 'lodger huts', accommodating 84 men in all, along with hut keepers and their families Each dwelling had a piped water supply, hot and cold washing facilities, bath and water-borne sanitation, all much superior to the style of the villages before the first

Upstream of the embankment site, an early erection was the temporary north catchwater viaduct of 1930-31. It is seen carrying 2ft gauge tracks over Black Cleugh heading up dale for 2½ miles, to lay a piped catchwater from (far away left) Killhope and Wellhope burns, into the eventual reservoir. Cleugh House (roof) is seen in foreground. Black Cleugh hamlet is in the trees ahead.

In (probably) August 1931, the valve tower is rising rapidly and this extensive vista westward, up-stream, is achieved from its top. The cut-off trench for the embankment's foundations crosses left to right in foreground. A temporary gap remains for the residual waters of the Burnhope burn but the main flow is seen newly diverted just this side of the old road bridge, to reach a straight channel (crossed by 2ft gauge railway bridge); the channel gives access to outlet valve and draw-off apparatus in the valve tower, with tunnel beneath the embankment site. The two up-valley railway routes, also depicted on our map, are prominent. Whin Sike quarry is still to be developed in the left hillside, ahead. Burnhope Plantation quarry is glimpsed, top right, and the 1 in 5 (approx.) incline (standard gauge, later narrow gauge) is bringing down the stone for crushing and concrete making. Holme House farm is in middle distance and Hill End's hayricks in the field up to its left.

world war. The domestic supply reservoir (40,000 gallons) was on a stream immediately north of the embankment and the sewage works was near the burn downstream of the new construction works. The canteen included a social room, billiard room, cinema hall and reading room. Relatively isolated, away up the hill and commanding the embankment site from its north end, the 'reservoir house' was erected, 1930-31, for the resident engineer and in the long term for the D.C.W.B. resident bailiff.

Preliminary works and main excavation.

As usual, a priority was diversion of the main stream in the valley. The diversion tunnel was constructed during 1930-31, completed October 1931. 2ft gauge railways removed spoil at each end of the tunnel. The valve shaft was sunk from ground level to the tunnel at this time to provide intermediate access and speed the tunnel works. The 30in water supply pipe (in use, it will be recalled as a temporary supply from the burn to the Board's area) was diverted below the tunnel and eventually the main outlet pipes from the valve tower were to pass through the tunnel.

In August 1930 demolition commenced of the hamlet of Burnhope, located along the rough lane, which crossed the burn by a three arch stone bridge just upstream of the main dam site. Cottages and farm were taken down, indeed six farmsteads in the valley were dismantled, and the stone transported for re-use. This work was completed by the end of 1931. Excavation of the 'cut-off trench' across the valley on the centre line of the dam was begun early in 1931 and largely completed, without incident, in May 1932; its maximum depth was 147ft below the valley floor and average 95ft, length 2002ft, while Oregon pine was imported for its timbering. Pressure grouting of the rock into which the trench locks was undertaken; borings were taken to 80ft maximum depth and 185 tons of cement were injected.

Plantation quarry, railway incline and concrete plant.

Concrete was required for the tunnel works and then in quantity for filling the cut-off trench to ground level. Bagged cement was brought by rail to the Board's sidings at Wearhead station and thence by motor lorries to the cement store at site. A major quarry had to be opened up to secure stone suitable for crushing for aggregate to make concrete. Burnhope Plantation quarry was developed at 1570ft o.d., high up the hillside north west of the dam site, to provide stone suitable for aggregate and sand. It remains impressive today and a scramble up to it is rewarded by a bird's eye view of the dam and its approaches. Standard gauge tracks were laid in this quarry and on a double track incline down through the plantation and almost into the bottom of the valley - thus running below the water level of today's lake. Due to this fact and also the felling and replanting of the plantation in circa 1944, it is by no means easy to locate precisely the line of the incline; the resident engineer's map of the site and viewing from the embankment

Holme House farm and barns are now in close-up, thought to be after the days of Farmer Edgar Robinson and with site staff in occupation, washing out while the weather keeps fair. At least eight narrow gauge steam locomotives can be discerned, with the vista generally opening out downstream towards the embankment works.

Rather later, with valvetower and embankment seen rising, and some stone 'pitching' already on the water face, we have a fine close-up of old Burnhope bridge. A small loco is passing, right, betrayed by steam.

A load of 'fill' has been brought by loco No.70 (purpose built in 1931 by Andrew Barclay of Kilmarnock) to the dam embankment site and is being discharged. Observe the lighting to permit 'late shift'.

More 'fill' to form the body of the dam embankment is being tipped near the interlocking with the valley side, believed at the south end of the dam. 81 DURHAM is one of the pretty side tank engines built by Avonside for Burnhope, in 1933.

top have made possible its delineation on our map. The control of loaded wagons descending from Plantation quarry was achieved by connection of the winch at the head of the incline to an 'engine' which in turn drove an air compressor and charged an air vessel, from which compressed air was drawn for site needs, presumably including air-driven tools in the quarry itself. The load provided by the compressor kept down the speed of the 'engine' and thus of the winch and the haulage rope. It was reported that the 'engine' could alternatively be driven by compressed air in order to exercise more positive control of the winch.

M.S.C. type standard gauge wagons were used in the quarry, moved around by horses and manually. At the incline foot the contents of the wagons was tipped into a steel chute feeding a two-stage stone crushing plant, driven by two 65 h.p. motors. At an uncertain date, the rails on the incline were closed in to convert the tracks to 2ft gauge and track in the quarry was converted to mixed gauge (standard and 2ft). Hudson steel wagons of 1 cu yd capacity were then used on the narrow gauge for conveying the stone to the crusher. A surviving photograph provides evidence of the use of locomotives in the quarry, but this is believed to be after conversion of the incline to narrow gauge.

Trains of twelve 1 cu yd wagons ran on 2ft gauge from the crushing plant to the concrete mixers, of which four were installed (two ¾ cu yd capacity rotary drum mixers by Ransomes and two smaller ones). The pre-measured (batched) content of each wagon in the trains from the stone crushing and sand plant to the mixers was tipped into the chutes at the mixers. Mixed concrete was discharged from the plant into crane skips having hinged bottom doors. These were mounted on bogies and moved to the required location on the tunnels, valveshaft and other concrete work. The plant was resited accessibly to the cut-off trench for the immediately ensuing work of placing concrete in the trench, this last between April 1932 and the end of February 1933. The south arm trench was filled somewhat later. To handle the skips of concrete for the trench, 5-tons capacity steam cranes ran on 7ft gauge tracks in the valley bottom and these cranes had also played their part in the earlier excavation of the trench. At a later stage still, one of the mixers was located close by the crushing plant and crocodile wagons, of a design evolved at site, ran on the 2ft gauge, each carrying five skips (3 cu yds in all) of mixed concrete direct to points where it was needed, for immediate placing. All these trains were hauled by small steam locomotives, of which more anon.

Glimpsed (right) is 82 WEAR of the Avonside design while focal is 77 KILLHOPE 0-4-2 saddle tank by Kerr Stuart, 1908 (of their TATTOO class). This is believed to be by the concrete mixer, itself fed from the crushing plant adjoining. A bogie wagon carries skips for liquid concrete, each with lifting lugs for handling by rail-mounted crane, and with bottom doors to release the charge.

Let us now come closer to site operations at the peak of the job. A Ruston Bucyrus internal-combustion 'navvy' is excavating 'fill' material and loading it into small Jubilee rail skips. The old bridge is seen; the immediate job may be river diversion.

More quarries and their access routes.

On the south side of the valley, in the south east bank of the Whin Sike inlet, about 50ft below eventual top water level, a quarry was developed to provide stone for beaching the lower slopes of the embankment water face - in crazy-paving style - and pitching the upper portion - in square blocks. All this stone was brought out on 2ft gauge.

For building of boundary walls around the hillsides, stone was secured from a small quarry, still visible today, in the south side of the valley immediately downstream of the embankment and close to it, with narrow gauge rail access. This was known as Howe's quarry, after the man in charge.

Shap granite was imported, by rail, then by lorry from Wearhead station, for finishing off major masonry works. Quarrymen and masons are understood to have been recruited mainly from the Silent Valley scheme in Ireland.

The dam at Burnhope - spoil, railways, rollers.

The forming of the huge dam embankment was a lengthy job and extended from the beginning of 1933 to mid-1935. Shale and boulder clay for this purpose were dug out in Whin Sike. There were at site five Ruston Bucyrus internal combustion excavators, the day of the steam navvy being over. The two of greatest capacity, Ruston 37 RB diesel excavators each with 1½ cu yd bucket, worked at Whin Sike getting fill and loading it into the trains of 2ft gauge steel tip wagons. These trains had to be worked to the bank over a route where undulations of 1 in 35 and steeper predominated. The locomotives were hard put to on this work. Some 1.6 million cu yds of material was shifted to form the bank, hardly surprising when one views its bulk, now softened to the eye by the grass, towering up the side valley above Wearhead.

Three steam rollers were used for the progressive consolidation of the embankment as it was built up by tipping from the narrow gauge trucks -

One Fowler 10 tons Council type roller, but with slightly enlarged rolls and serrated tyres, and low geared.

One T. Green 13 tons roller of comparable type, similarly modified.

One Marshall (of Gainsborough) specially developed roller, weight 16 tons light and 17 tons in working order. The back rolls, ribbed, were each 3ft wide and no less than 10ft diameter, as high as the long canopy. The front rolls, smooth, were each 2ft 6in wide and 7ft diameter but separated by 5ft 6in to enable the machine to roll astride a 2ft gauge railway track. This roller was powered by a Sentinel boiler, working pressure 275 p.s.i., and Sentinel engine, rated at 126 h.p. for short periods, with two speed gearbox, giving low gearing, and having the refinement of steam steering. It could roll directly up and down a gradient of 1 in 3 in course of consolidating the water face of the embankment prior to pitching. Again, it could, on the level, start away on newly tipped wet clay, such was its adhesion. Its 2ft ground clearance permitted working in soft material long after the other rollers (with fireboxes 6in above the ground) had to give up. Indeed, its output was more than double either of the others. When the time came to part, it was agreed, on 17 March 1936, that it be delivered to the South Essex Waterworks Company, Abberton, for £425.

It has been stated that a Sentinel steam lorry, with specially heavy chassis, was used at Burnhope, presumably on the road haulage from the station (although this is discounted), and that this too went to the South Essex Company.

Puddle clay and its transport.

Concurrently with the creation of the embankment came, as usual, the demand for clay puddle for the core. An adequate supply was most conveniently found in the hillside immediately north of the embankment site and the digging out of the hillside in this area produced an excavation which, landscaped and turfed, has created a handsome amphitheatre at bank-top height which - but for the low Pennine temperatures at over 1300ft o.d., could be visualised as setting the scene for summer evening concert or theatrical performances. The clay was accessible but unfortunately it was burdened with 42-45 per cent of stone, varying from boulders to gravel, when the mechanical excavator first dug it out of the hillside. The gang working with the excavator received a bonus for the measure of excavated stone separated from the clay. Temporary narrow gauge tracks were used for the wagons of clay to the pugmill, which was located on the edge of the excavated area by the north end of the bank. Here the smaller stones and gravel were picked out during cutting up on a long stage and feeding by conveyor along the staging, where boy pickers were at work, again remunerated according to the cubic measure of stone secured - which was itself cleared away

After concrete comes clay for the water-resistant core of the dam. Brought from the puddle-clay field, it is being tipped and fed by gravity to the pugmill. A Kerr Stuart 0-4-0 saddle tank of 'Wren' class to the left is likely to be GNAT or WASP.

Pugged clay, received by train from the mill, is being tipped from Jubilee skips, eased down chutes, shovelled into place, stamped home and rammed with a 'petrol punner' (displayed to the observer). The train on the left, with loco, is delivering and tipping 'fill', to give body to the embankment.

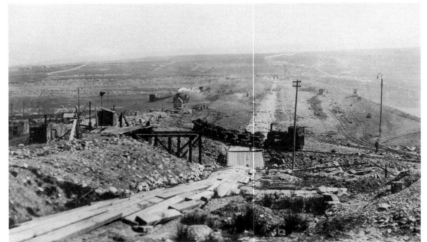

Viewing from up at the reservoir house, above the bank's north west end, the scene is directly across the puddle trench. Loco-hauled traffics and the big Marshall roller are seen. The Kerr Stuart 0-4-2 saddle tank loco in foreground is seemingly on clay duties.

Coming down to look more closely, here is a moment of drama! The Marshall steam roller is on a 1 in 4 gradient, charging the upstream (west) slope of the embankment - compacting it. The intrepid driver is Lawson Featherstone, a local Wearhead man, who earlier drove steam wagons for the Bradley Brothers. Stanley Allderidge has introduced water ballast to the very large wheels to achieve his demanded adhesion.

by rail from a convenient 'stone siding'. The clay passed through two successive sets of rolls, with more hand picking between them, then - watered - to the actual bladed pugmill, from which it was discharged into the usual 1 cu yd steel tip wagons on a 2ft gauge track beneath the mill. The loaded wagons of clay were lowered by winch down an incline from top bank level at the north end to, initially, the valley bottom, where the wagons were tipped onto cutting-up stages alongside the core trench; the clay was cut into pigs, which were delivered to the core down watered chutes, much after the manner adopted at Scout Dike (Penistone) a few years earlier, then trodden and heeled in, layer by layer. When the bank eventually rose to about half its height, locomotive working of the clay trucks from pugmill down to bank top was substituted for the winch and incline.

Finishing off the embankment.

As the bank rose, the beaching (begun June 1932) and the pitching (placed from May 1935) were carried on until completion towards the end of 1935. The valvetower was only built in this latter era and finished in March 1936. The overflow weir and channels, turfing and fencing were completed about this time.

Catchwaters and a light railway.

An integral part of the Engineers' design of the Burnhope project was the impounding of waters, not only from the Burnhope stream but from the many tributary burns and sykes which flowed into the valley, also from a vast number of streams which were tapped by construction of the north and south catchwaters.

The north catchwater, 2½ miles long, originated at an intake on the Wellhope burn immediately upstream of its junction with Killhope burn, most of the Wellhope water being drawn off. It tapped twelve minor streams en route, passing on its way close by houses titled Blakeleyfield, The Rush, High Allers, The Hill, The Berts and below Cleugh House but above the byroad and The Locks. This catchwater involved excavation, cut and cover, and laying pipes, also the construction of the intakes and a syphon. A 2ft gauge light railway, using one or more internal combustion locomotives, paralleled the excavation during this work, period around May 1930 to September 1931. Much of the route of this line can be seen, including evidence of footings of the trestle bridge across Black Cleugh (and a pipebridge on the deviation, with syphon, just downstream of this trestle). In the head of Black Cleugh, it is interesting to observe Cleugh House, a traditional byre, with living quarters on the floor above it and a garret in the gable above these - but it is no longer occupied as a house.

The south catchwater was 5½ miles long, tapping the Ireshopeburn, West Grain, East Grain, Daddry Shields burn and twenty-five lesser streams. Owing to the uneven route, no railway was employed. The pipes were fitted with wooden discs and rolled by diesel tractors across the rough slopes, the work being completed around August 1932, with little damage to pipelengths. Four syphons were constructed on this catchwater. Two early Fordson petrol tractors figured in cut-and-cover on soft ground for (primarily) the south catchwater.

For road use at and to site, the Board owned a Trojan lorry, a sturdy make of the time. Small Bedford lorries also appeared, these belonging to cartage contractor Corbett, who came in from Sheffield and established himself in Weardale.

Completion and inauguration of supply.

The labour force rose to about 570 men by the end of March 1933 and 700 by the end of 1934, followed by a steady decrease to 150 at the close of 1935 and a further run down in 1936. Mr Stanley Allderidge resigned at 31 December 1935, taking up an appointment as resident engineer to the South Essex Waterworks Company on the construction of Abberton reservoir, south of Colchester. His deputy, L.H. Brown, was in charge through the year 1936. He had lived until then at West Black Dene, just downstream of Wearhead village, but he occupied the 'reservoir house' through 1936, resigning from his appointment at December 1936; the house was then reconditioned for long-term occupation by the D.C.W.B. official in charge of the operational reservoir.

A Ruston Bucyrus diesel-powered excavator with 1½ cu yd capacity bucket is in Whin Sike quarry, probably in 1934-35. Limestone is here extracted for beaching and pitching the water face of the embankment. 'Fill' was earlier secured from this quarry.

John Peadon (Mr Peadon Senior to me) had been employed by the Water Board in charge of the completed and operational pipeline from an intake at Burnhope down to its Stanhope tunnel during the latter half of the 1920s. Through the Burnhope construction era he was the Board's 'man on the site' at Burnhope with an administrative role and access to Durham headquarters. From 1936 he was appointed reservoir keeper, styled bailiff, and around mid 1937 took over the reservoir house for himself and family. He was thus in charge until retirement in 1958, and indeed resided in the house for a year or two beyond that. His son, Fred Peadon, was bailiff in succession from 1958 until 1965, occupying the reservoir house until 1969. He transferred to wider ranging appointments for the Board and acquired his own present residence in North Grain, Wearhead. I owe much to the pleasure of meeting his father and enjoying the recollections and guidance of Fred Peadon; map-making by Arthur Chambers likewise benefited enormously. Mr Chrimes was an assistant engineer who saw the constructional job through at Burnhope. He went on to appointment as resident engineer of Corby District Water Company in Northamptonshire for constructing Corby (Eyebrook) reservoir, 1937-40 - accompanied by four narrow gauge steam locomotives from the Burnhope stock. He was a lively figure, of maybe some independent means; he resided in a country hotel in Allendale and drove daily to and from Burnhope in his M.G. sports car - over the intermediate mountain road and its 1850ft summit.

Also in Whin Sike quarry, stone dressers and steam locomotives, at least three locos, are all active in the wider scene.

Partial filling of the reservoir was authorised by September 1935 and filling to overflowing accomplished by April 1936. The final certificate of completion was dated 25 August 1936.

In June 1936 it was decided to raze and dispose of the buildings of the temporary reservoir village, except the recreation hall and two lesser structures. The timber locomotive shed was eventually acquired by a farmer and it could still be seen in his fields on the lower side of the byroad between Cowshill and the embankment, in 1977, if viewed through the eye of faith. Progressive collapse had reached the stage where the decrepit gable was standing on the ground.

The agreement between the Board and the L.N.E.R. for sidings at Wearhead, dating from 19 January 1926, was terminated from 2 September 1935. In a letter of 14 October 1936, the L.N.E.R. agreed to reduce the charge for their abandonment from £199 to £56 in consideration of the retention by them, the Railway Company, of the materials recovered in lifting.

Sales of plant were effected in 1934, 1935, 1936 and later. The locomotives did not sell readily and in fact were not all sold until later in 1937 or early in 1938; the evidence on this will be mentioned later. From time to time John Peadon would steam a locomotive to shunt newly sold locos ready for loading and despatch.

The formal opening ceremony was held over until 16 September 1937, by which time railways and most buildings had been cleared away and the site largely landscaped. A special train ran at 10.12am from Bishop Auckland, calling at stations to Wearhead, to convey guests to the ceremony. Sadly, Peter Lee had died in office in 1935; he had been dedicated to the success of the project and welfare of the workers. Inauguration was by Eli Cook, J.P., by now chairman of D.C.W.B. Henry Robinson was still the Board's own engineer but on 8 July 1933 he had suffered severe injury in a motor accident; not until 15 January 1935 could he attend at site and was even then not fully recovered and he resigned on 30 April 1938, when J. Arthur Rodwell from the Irwell Valley Water Board took over. The occasion of the opening in September 1937 was marked by a storm of rain and wind; the guests were no doubt glad to retire to Wearhead and join the returning special train at 2.45pm.

The engineer to the Sunderland and South Shields Water Company at the time of the opening was Alfred B.E. Blackburn. It should be mentioned that his Company built its own filter plant downstream of the Burnhope reservoir village and laid mains from there to their territory in order to carry the treated water, unlike D.C.W.B who took raw water from the reservoir to distant filters.

The waters began to engulf Burnhope bridge in August 1935. It is a happy thought here to place - Left - Henry Robinson, engineer and manager of Durham County Water Board from its formation, 1920. With stick - Peter Lee, Councillor, J.P., a long-time Durham miners' leader, elected chairman of the County Council in 1920 and also from then chairman of D.C.W.B. and their ladies. Peter Lee cut the first sod at Burnhope, 18 July 1930, but sadly died in 1935 before inauguration.

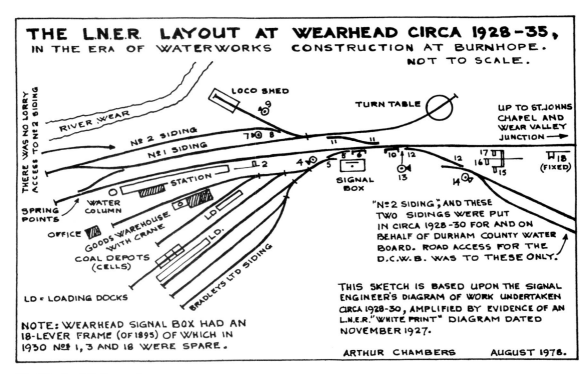

The Wearhead Railway - footnotes.

A visit on 10 April 1936, in company with the Wearhead station master of the L N.E.R., to the neat little yellowish brick locomotive shed on the very fringe of railway property beside the river Wear, revealed No.314. This was a J21 class 0-6-0 locomotive, built by the N.E.R. at Gateshead in 1890, enjoying a day of rest : it was Good Friday, here devoid of train service, as on Sundays.

At this period, six passenger trains each way served Wearhead, Monday-Friday, with seven on Saturday. Prior to 8 July 1935, when Wear Valley Junction station and engine shed closed, the Wearhead engine (which for long was a 0-4-4 Tank of class G5) had run the passenger trains only as far as the Junction, but by 1935-36 the J21 was working -

Early turn men: 6.35am Wearhead to Bishop Auckland/ Sunderland (9.9am)

10.0am Sunderland to Bishop Auckland/ Wearhead (1.12pm)

Afternoon goods, Wearhead to Westgate and back.

Late turn men: 3.35pm Wearhead to Bishop Auckland / Darlington (5.11pm)

7.28pm Darlington to Bishop Auckland

9.8pm Bishop Auckland to Wearhead (10.12pm, the end of the day).

The other workings into Wearhead were stated to involve West Auckland power and men and one each way was undertaken by a Sentinel steam railcar. Wearhead to Westgate was being operated 'one engine in steam'. Wearhead maintained no stock of locomotive coal in 1936 and the engine was liable to be changed over at Darlington for maintenance. Nevertheless, Arthur Camwell captured 314, by then L.N.E.R. 5064, at Wearhead on 7 May 1948 - photographed on the 2.30pm passenger train for Darlington, presumably successor to the 3.35pm of 1936. The little engine shed, opened 1895 with the branch, closed 29 June 1953, when the whole branch closed to regular passenger trains, and Tom Rounthwaite believed that 314 (later in turn 5064 and 65064) was in general the Wearhead engine right through from October 1935 to 1953.

Although final freight closure to Wearhead took effect at 2 January 1961, the track was still down at Autumn 1963, with wagons stored upon it west of St. John's Chapel, the then terminus. St. John's Chapel to Westgate (exclusive) closed from 1 November 1965 and was lifted by September 1966. From Westgate (inclusive) to the new cement works of A.P.C.M. Limited (located about a half mile west of Eastgate station and opened in 1965) the branch closed from 1 July 1968. It has remained open until 1993 for traffic to and from the cement works, while passenger trains still operate between Bishop Auckland and Darlington. Eastgate station closed to normal goods traffic w.e.f. 7 July 1980, no goods going beyond Wolsingham after that time.

In 1961 the station and yard at Wearhead were occupied by A. Corbett & Son (Wearhead) Limited, as an office and base for lorries. The locomotive shed was then standing but its single road had been lifted, probably for many years. By 1977, although devoid of track, the station area had in most respects changed greatly for the better. J. Hodson (Wearhead) Limited are in occupation. The firm's busy agency for Landrovers, the staple transport of the district, occupies the frontage to the road, with neat new buildings. A stone loading bank can be found in the former yard area. The brick goods shed has been restored as a store for horses' fodder. The wall of the station buildings facing onto the passenger platform has been adapted and a handsome bungalow residence built behind it for the principal of the owners, with its main elevation towards the approach drive and lawns. The former station master's brick house, where I was hospitably received in 1936, remains, tidy and lived in, close beside the entrance gates to the drive from road to station. The locomotive shed has been demolished.

Wearhead station from its dead end in British Railways' days - 65068, N.E.R. 0-6-0 class J21 was built in 1890 at Darlington, N.E.R. 300, and withdrawn in 1954; it has arrived with a passenger train and is taking water before running round and turning.

From the outer end, 65092 of the same class J21, onetime No. 1565, built 1891 at Gateshead, also eventually withdrawn in 1954, is being turned between passenger trips, 6 April 1953. The signal box is seen still in full use.

L.N.E.R. 5064, previously 314, another J21 engine, this one of 1890 Gateshead and 1958 withdrawal, a regular engine at Wearhead 1935-53, is on 2.30pm passenger to Darlington, 7 May 1948.

N.E.R./L.N.E.R. 1566 (later becoming 5093), also of class J21, dated from 1891 at Gateshead to 1949, poses for Arthur Camwell outside the charming engine shed at Wearhead, close above the river, in the 1930's.

The vast Kielder water impounding scheme in former Border Counties Railway (N.B.R.) territory embraced construction of aqueduct tunnels on generally north-to-south alignment. The route as glimpsed here, 8 June 1980, cuts across Weardale between Stanhope (left) and Frosterley (right). The B.R. line is seen running down the dale, left to right, with the narrow gauge tunnel burrowing northward beneath it.

Standard gauge locomotives of D.C.W.B on Burnhope project

As explained in the account already given, no rail link was in the event constructed from Wearhead station to the reservoir site area at Burnhope. The limited s.g. layout which emerged was an anachronism and even then only in use for about three years, perhaps slightly less.

Quotations were obtained from Hunslet Engine Company of Leeds for two s.g. locomotives, on 3 March 1931 -

> 0-6-0 Saddle tank oc 12in x 18in,
> described by the makers as similar to GILMORE HE597/1893 for Liverpool United Gas Company.
>
> 0-4-0 Saddle tank oc 10in x 15in,
> 'similar to VIKING HE 1293/1918 for Wigan Rolling Mills C. Ltd.'

The two locomotives actually secured by the Board were -

> 0-6-0 Saddle tank oc 14in x 22in
> by Avonside Engine Co. 2000 of 1930 - came new
> Disposal was in c 8/1934 (to) Newbiggin Colliery Co. Ltd., Northumberland - once called their TEDDY, surviving until 1964 for N.C.B. at this location.
>
> 0-4-0 Saddle tank oc 12in x 20in
> by Andrew Barclay 1988 of 1931 - came new
> Disposal was via the agency of Central Wagon Company, a Wigan firm, to Cambrian Wagon Works Ltd., Maindy Works, Cardiff, in 10/1933 - surviving until at least 1958.

The 2ft gauge locomotives engaged on the Burnhope project of D.C.W.B.

A composite table of these narrow gauge locomotives has been created and is presented, numbered in serial order between 1 and 87, 23 in all. This is preceded below by supplementary comments on their acquisition; then as to their employment (supplementing the main text); and on disposals.

A few comments on acquisition of the locomotives

Having determined to work primarily with 2ft gauge steam locomotives - on a site providing a tough assignment - the Water Board had to show flexibility, securing new and second-hand engines according to availability. In June-December 1932 one second-hand loco came for as little as £140 but new locos at 'up to £600 each' were also in mind. In later years, Tom Shand, of Lehane, Mackenzie & Shand, claimed to W.J. Dyer of Hastings Corporation to have been instrumental in selling some of the 'Tattoo' 0-4-2 Tanks of antiquity to the Water Board, presumably on behalf of Pugsleys of Bristol. Late in purchases, the water committee was displeased (19 December 1933) at the purchase of two locomotives at £250 (the pair?) without prior reference to them by the joint engineers.

Locomotive operation

Mr Stanley S. Allderidge, the resident engineer - the chief at site - noted in his paper of 1935 on the overall project that during the busy periods no spare locos were available. He commented that the excavated 'fill' from Whin Syke to the embankment (to form the latter) was hauled by steam locos of 7½ and 8 tons weight on 2ft gauge. Broadly this fits the locos by Andrew Barclay, Avonside Engine Company and 0-4-2 Tanks by Kerr Stuart. Kenneth Allderidge, schoolboy in the days of the job but a chief in his own right in Essex in postwar years, told me that the shale, namely 'fill' for the bank, was mainly handled by Kerr Stuart 0-4-2 saddle tanks. He also said that MIDGE and GNAT (Kerr Stuart 'Wrens') ran from clayfield to pugmill with puddle clay and that Sentinel and Barclay ran from pugmill to trench. Mr Peadon Senior, talking in Weardale in 1961, added that MIDGE, GNAT and WASP ('Wrens') were known at site as 'Coffeepots' and were on duty in connection with the puddle-clay plant, while the Sentinel and the Fowler (a six-coupled engine) ran from the puddle plant to the trench - the remainder mostly hauling 'muck' (fill) for forming the dam. All the above accords broadly.

Disposals

'Supplementaries' include -

31/12/1935	Various plant has been sold to South Essex Waterworks Company.
17/3/1936	The sale of the Marshall steam roller, delivered at Abberton, South Essex Waterworks Company, has been agreed at £425.

Plant sales have totalled -   by end of 1934 -   £2,729
　　　　　　　　　　　　　　"　　　　" 　1935 -   £4,841
　　　　　　　　　　　　　　"　　　　3/1936 -   £12,435 some plant remaining for sale

20/10/1936	The locos for sale are to be advertised in trade journals.
15/12/1936	Locos - more favourable offers are hoped for and the engineer is to take steps to prevent their deterioration due to exposure to the weather (N.B. The loco shed had been dismantled 'as part of the tidying and landscaping.')
16/2/1937	Birtley Brick Co. Ltd. have offered £140 for loco No. 83; the Board are asking £150. (N.B. It was sold to them in that year).
16/3/1937	The engineer has at this date received an offer for 6 locos but one had been received prior to this (presumably meaning Birtley's offer for No. 83 - and our schedule shows various earlier sales). The engineer is to pursue the sale of the 5 locos at present for disposal: presumed the last five and I would think the four which went to Corby (Eyebrook reservoir) and No. 75 WELLHOPE KS 1145/1912 which eventually went to Hunslet Company, believed in 1938; these sales seem to have been effected between 9/1937 and 2/1938.
15/2/1938	The sale of the locos at Burnhope reported realising £490 (meaning, presumably, the sale of the last five, or less, and implying all sold at last).

It was clearly significant for sale of locos (and other plant) that Stanley Allderidge, resident engineer at Burnhope, resigned on 31 December 1935 on taking up a similar appointment at Abberton, for 'South Essex'. Likewise, Mr Chrimes, an assistant engineer through the Burnhope job, moved at its close to take charge of the Corby (Eyebrook) reservoir construction and figures above 'acquiring' four steam locos from Weardale. Overall, the steam locomotives went as follows: -

to Cliffe Hill Granite	1
South Essex, Abberton	6
Penrhyn Quarries	5
Cohens	1
Birtley Brick	1
Corby (Eyebrook)	4
Waltons' Limestone, Alston	1
Hunslet of Leeds	_2_
	21 and two i/c locos disposed of earlier.

2ft gauge locomotive 3, also known as GREEN, by Andrew Barclay 1855 of 1931, was the makers' first 0-4-0 well tank, 7in x 11 in cylinders, supplied new to the site and is posed for Barclays. The side-tipper skip wagons are understood to be by Hudson of Leeds, each 1 cu yd capacity, and likely also to be supplied for DCWB.

No.5, known as GREY, AB 1994/1931 figures with No.70 (maybe BLACK) AB 1995/1931, and another of the same type - all akin to 3 and comprising a Barclay 'official' view, probably just on arrival, as Burnhope site locomotive shed is in the background.

2ft gauge locomotives of Durham County Water Board : Burnhope project

Plant No. and name at Burnhope	Type Cyls (in inches) builder	Prior history, and at this site.	History subsequent to its stay at Burnhope site.
1	4 wheels petrol 20hp Simplex 5067/1930	came new	Minute 24/5/1932: on reco. of the junior engineers, D.C.W.B. decided to dispose of the petrol locomotive plant and purchase two second-hand steam locos at £135 each.
2	4 wheels petrol 20hp Simplex 5132/1930	came new	(Purchase of locos 79 and 80, of which see details below, appears likely, probably through agents).
3 GREEN	0-4-0WT oc 7 x 11 7½ tons AB 1855/1931	came new	Disposal to Corby District Water Co., Eyebrook resr. job 1937-40; with Pugsley 1940; later Roads Reconstruction Ltd., Grovesend Quarry, Tytherington, 11/1941; by 11/1948 dumped there off track/lay at Co.'s Cranmore Depot subsequently, where B/U 1959.
4 RED	0-4-0WT oc 7 x 11 7½ tons AB 1991/1931	came new	Disposal to Penrhyn Quarries Ltd, Bethesda, in 10/1936, becoming CEGIN; resold to USA, shipped 3/1965.
5 GREY	0-4-0WT oc 7 x 11 7½ tons AB 1994/1931	came new	Disposal to Penrhyn Quarries Ltd, Bethesda, in 1/1938, becoming GLYDER; resold to USA, shipped 3/1965.
6 (maybe EDITH)	4 wheels Tank VB 6 tons Sentinel 6902/1927	came ex (or via) J.C. Oliver, dealer, Leeds	Disposal to Cliffe Hill Granite Co. Ltd, Markfield, Leics (in 1935 ?), becoming EDITH - out of use there by 1947 and B/U 1957
70 (maybe BLACK)	0-4-0WT oc 7 x 11 7½ tons AB 1995/1931	came new	Disposal to Corby District Water Co., Eyebrook resr. job, 1937-40; later with F.W. Dobson & Co. Ltd., Raisby Hill Lime Works, Coxhoe Bridge, working as 'No. 70 'until replaced by i/c locos; then resold 7/1948 to Dinorwic Quarries Ltd. and worked at Port Dinorwic; sold again 8/1962 to Hampshire Narrow Gauge Preservation Society, near Eastleigh; but again sold - to J.M. Baldock, of Liphook, by 6/1971 for Hollycombe Woodland Garden Railway.
72 MIDGE	0-4-0ST oc 6 x 9 5 tons 'Wren' class KS 4290/1923	had been new 2/1923 to R.H. Neal, hirers and suppliers, of Ealing, at Dartford/passing via Clarkson of Wigan in 7/1931 to Nelson Corpn, Coldwell Resr; thence acquired in (believed) 5/1932 by D.C.W.B.	Disposal to South Essex Waterworks Company, Abberton, Colchester in 1/1936; resold 1939 to A.P.C.M. Ltd., Holborough Cement Works, Kent, but disappeared there about 1940, still unused at that site.

No.70 is still very smart and polished, but on duty, 19 February 1932, although near the engine sheds, with glimpse of lodger huts to the north. Some 40 years later this loco found its way to the Hollycombe Woodland Garden Railway, a more secluded site in south country.

75 WELLHOPE 0-4-2 saddletank 7in x 12in KS 1145/1912 of the makers' 'Tattoo' class started life on reservoir work near Portsmouth. It is seen weatherworn at the end of the Burnhope job. It went on to a career in East African sugar.

73 GNAT	0-4-0ST oc 6 x 9 5 tons 'Wren' class KS 4291/1923	had been new 4/1923 to Neal as above (? for Sir Wm. Arrol on Dartford Bypass constrn)/passing via Clarkson of Wigan in 7/1931 to Nelson Corpn, Coldwell Resr; thence acquired in (believed) 7/1932 by D.C.W.B.	Disposal to South Essex Waterworks Company, Abberton, Colchester in 1/1936; they offered it for sale 12/1938; HE Coy. show it with R.H. Bolton & Co., Birmingham at 28/3/1939; maybe for Quants reservoir, Somerset circa 3/1939 - 2/1941. It passed to Paulings, who may have used it on Pembrey ROF contract from c.1942 - lying at Paulings' Danygraig depot by 1948 and B/U there in 1950.
74 BURNHOPE	0-4-2ST oc 7 x 12 8½ tons 'Tattoo' class KS 1144/1911	ordered 20/9/1911 and new 30/9/1911 to Fareham station LSWR Likely to work for Mowlems (No.25) (who had private siding, Farlington, LBSCR, NE from Portsmouth) on Farlington resrs and filter beds (and prob. MM factory nearby); among 13 locos offered by Geo. Cohen & Armstrong Disposal Corpn, Farlington 23/7/26. Came to DCWB ex Pugsley of Bristol (dealers) as SG 721 by 7/1932.	Offered for sale by DCWB 28/1/1936 (after prob. repairs by HE Co. Ltd.) - disposal to South Essex Waterworks Co., Abberton prob. early in 1936; thence resold in late 1938 or 1939 to Hastings Corpn, for Darwell Hole reservoir (and recalled by res. engineers at both these sites) - and believed B/U 5/1951 for Hastings.
75 WELLHOPE	0-4-2ST oc 7 x 12 8½ tons 'Tattoo' class KS 1145/1912	ordered 29/12/1911 and new 27/1/1912 to Fareham station LSWR; at 7/2/1912 Mowlems (their No.20) engineer claimed wheels one in. different from their other locos; prob. similar history to KS1144 down to 7/1926; came as above from Pugsley SG720 in 7/1932.	for sale by DCWB 28/1/1936 (after prob. repairs by HE Co. Ltd.), disposal was to HE Coy in 1938, who resold it 10/1940 via one I. Gundle, to East African sugar factory.
76 IRESHOPE	0-4-2ST oc 7 x 12 8½ tons 'Tattoo' class KS 1142/1911	ordered 14/1/1910 new on 7/2/1911 poss. at Fareham LSWR. (Mowlems No.22) Prob. similar history to KS1144 down to 7/1926; came from Pugsley SG723 in 6/1932.	for sale by DCWB 28/1/1936 (after prob. repairs by HE Co. Ltd.); disposal to South Essex Waterworks Co., Abberton, prob. early in 1936; thence resold to Hastings Corpn, for Darwell Hole in 1938 or 1939 (and recalled by resr. engineers at both these sites) - and believed B/U 5/1951 for Hastings.
77 KILLHOPE	0-4-2ST oc 7 x 12 8½ tons 'Tattoo' class KS 1047/1908	built for stock new 1908 to Mowlems, lett'd as such at their Farlington siding. Prob. similar history to KS1144 down to 7/1926; came from Pugsley SG724 in c1931.	for sale by DCWB 28/1/1936 (after prob. repairs by HE Co. Ltd.) and sold by DCWB to HE Coy., in 1938, not traced thereafter- probably dismantled by HE.

79, never named by DCWB, is comparable with No. 70 but as AB 1453/1918 goes farther back, with an earlier history in airfield construction. It awaits disposal at the conclusion of Burnhope works - and later figures in the Pennine quarries near Alston.

84 AUCKLAND 0-4-0 side tank 7½in x 12in AE 2072/1933 is of the class for the job already illustrated at work and discussed in the text. Seen after completion, it still has to work in Northamptonshire, in Somerset, and then in India.

78 HARTHOPE	0-4-2ST oc 7 x 12 8½ tons 'Tattoo' class KS 1291/1915	new 8/2/1915 to Chief Supt. of Ordnance Factories for the building works dept.at Royal Arsenal, Woolwich. (in WD green livery). May have reached DCWB via Pugsley	for sale by DCWB 28/1/1936; disposal to South Essex Waterworks Co., Abberton, prob. early in 1936; to HE 1938; thence 1940 to Eastwoods Cement Company, Barrington, Cambridgeshire (but with H. Boot & Coy shown as being owners and/or contractors while at Eastwoods) - and B/U there c1948. after long disuse.
79	0-4-0WT oc 6¾ x 10¼ 7½ tons AB 1453/1918	new 4/4/1918 for Air Service Construction Corps' Hanworth Road Siding Sunbury, LSWR, lettered 'Air Construction Service 4' (on plates)/at Dymchurch Aerodrome by late 1918/ to RAF, Calshot in 11/1921/ thence in 1931 to AM. Works Dept, due heavy repairs (AB 1432 going to Calshot in its place); and to auction by Fuller Horsey & Co. 20/3/1931, acquired by DCWB.	Disposal in 1938 to Walton's Limestone Co., Alston (Quarries above top of incline on down side of LNER Alston branch, on nearing Alston station); a working engine there in 1939 - by 1961 quarry tracks disused here and no loco at site.
80	0-4-0ST oc 6 x 9 5 tons 'Wren' class KS 4001/1918	new 20/12/1918 at RAF Armaments School, Uxbridge, No.1, of Air Ministry; joining AB 1453/18 above at auction by Fuller Horsey & Co., 20/3/1931, acquired by D.C.W.B.	Disposal to South Essex Waterworks Company, Abberton, Colchester in probably 1/1936; thence offered for sale in 1938; and with R.H. Bolton & Co. of Birmingham; probably for Quants reservoir, Somerset circa 3/1939 - 2/1941, whence acquired 11/1942 by Paulings -who had it at their Danygraig yard by 1946; it lay dismantled there; B/U there 8/1950.
81 DURHAM	0-4-0 Side Tank oc 7 x 12 7½ tons steel firebox and belpaire; pedal and hand brakes, not steam. AE 2066/1933	came new	Disposal to Penrhyn Quarries Ltd, Bethesda, in 10/1936, becoming OGWEN; resold to USA, shipped 3/1965.
82 WEAR	0-4-0 Side Tank as above AE 2067/1933	came new	Disposal to Penrhyn Quarries Ltd, Bethesda, in 10/1936, becoming MARCHLYN; resold to USA, shipped 3/1965.
83 LANCHESTER	0-4-0 Side Tank oc 7½ x 12 7½ tons conventional brakes, hand and foot controls AE 2071/1933	came new	Disposal 1937 to Birtley Brick Co., Team Valley, retaining its painted number and name on service between claypit and kilns; seen here myself on down side of ECML 19/7/1945, out of use. Not visible passing 6/1946. Resold in 1948-49 via R.R.Dunn of Bishop Auckland to Dinorwic Quarries Ltd., Llanberis, becoming ELIDIR; resold to Canada in 1966.

85 SUNDERLAND AE 2073/1933 : here is an 'official' picture, before delivery to DCWB. The Belpaire firebox is *almost* concealed by the cab. Steam (to cylinders) and (as exhaust) from cylinders is prominently piped but the engine's outline is delightfully neat. Along with AUCKLAND, this one escaped the British preservationists and went off to India for cement manufacturers.

87 known as FOWLER at Burnhope 0-6-0 side tank 8½in x 12in by John Fowler 16991/1926 : a 'one off' loco at Burnhope, its earlier career having been in Lincolnshire chip-potato fields on the Nocton Estates Light Railway. It is seen disconsolate at the end of the work - believed languished until broken up here on site in 1938.

No.	Details	History	Disposal
84 AUCKLAND	0-4-0 Side Tank oc 7½ x 12 7½ tons brakes as above AE 2072/1933	came new	Disposal to Corby District Water Co., Eyebrook Resr., job 1937-40; later with Roads Reconstruction Ltd, Vallis Vale, Somerset, and subsequently at the Cranmore depot; thence 1951 via Oswald Bond, Cardiff (as 85 below)
85 SUNDERLAND	0-4-0 Side Tank oc 7½ x 12 7½ tons conventional brakes hand and int. expandg. foot controlled AE 2073/1933 Nos. 83-85 had Belpaire fireboxes like 81/2. All had external regulators mounted on the back of the dome. The extra half inch cylinder diameter of 83-85 was seemingly an 'afterthought'	came new	Disposal to Corby District Water Co., Eyebrook Resr., job 1937-40; later with Roads Reconstruction Ltd, at Grovesend Quarry, Tytherington; by 11/1948 dumped there off track and subsequently lay at Cranmore depot - with despatch via Cardiff as for AE 2072/1933. The boilers of both locos were rebuilt to the stringent Indian Boiler Regs. - as purchaser was Dalmia Cement Ltd., H.O. at New Delhi and with factories in the subcontinent.
86 STANHOPE	0-4-2 ST oc 7 x 12 8½ tons 'Tattoo' class KS 2395/1917	makers built it for stock from 12/1915 to achieve their first Hackworth valvegear and photo. New 23/2/1917 to Holloway Bros for Rosyth housing (1917-18) and Swanley roadworks (1922-24); they advertised it 4/1930. KS 2395/1917 to DCWB, their 86; its coming may have been under minute of 28/6/1932 to purchase an additional KS loco £140	Disposal by DCWB was to Penryhn Quarries Ltd., Bethesda in 12/1934, certainly by 1/1936, retaining name. It lay derelict Bethesda in 1950s to 1966, when dismantled. Talyllyn Rly. then secured some parts for their No.4 loco, stated stamped 2484 but one suspects more likely 2494 as 2484 was a KS loco abroad and 2494 had history with Trevor Granite, N. Wales.
87 Lettered N.E.L.P.	0-6-0 Side Tank oc 8½ x 12 11 tons John Fowler, Leeds 16991/1926	had been new 10/1926 to W. Dennis & Sons Ltd Lincs potato estates. Cohens ordered a chimney for it 5/1930, probably in course of sale / refurbishment for DCWB.	Disposal by DCWB : Cohens advertised it in 1937 and DCWB likewise in 1938 but evidently without a buyer and loco believed B/U at Burnhope site in 1938.

Footnote: In later years Raymond Dunn, of Bishop Auckland, much concerned in dealings with machinery, including industrial locos, recalled that the Board had latterly been desperate to sell their residual locomotives at Burnhope.

Alston station, exterior, 26 March 1967. Locomotive 43121 2-6-0 on tour train, from and to Glasgow.

Alston station, retaining overall roof : L.N.E.R. 7315 (former NER/LNER 2086) G5 0-4-4 tank on the 2.20pm for Haltwistle, with the loco shed glimpsed to right.

Lambley, showing also signal box, junction and the magnificent viaduct on the route to Haltwistle. Ahead at the divide is the NER/LNER to 'Lambley Fell', beyond which - on, westward - Lord Carlisle's Brampton Railway (then) continued the route.

Chapter Four
Bound for Geltsdale

Wearhead to Alston

The tale of 'Durham's Dales' brought us eastward over the high ridge at Killhope to reach Wearhead. Retracing one's steps by this 2056ft dalehead road, some six miles westward of Wearhead is the bleak hamlet of Nenthead; in my mind this is forever associated with the intriguing title of business clients in the 1930s. They were the Vieille Montagne Zinc Company. It seems that there had long been mining hereabouts for lead when this Company in 1896 set about exploiting zinc in the same hills. Their two or three narrow gauge locomotives appear to have been, to say the least, peculiar.

After four more miles of descent, one enters the top of Alston, which liked to be known as 'the highest market town in England'. One can still bump down its contorted and cobbled street and market place to the railway station.

Alston's railways

Alston station is at about 900ft o.d. The imposing stone building used to provide its station master with spacious residence above the offices. The roof which extended from the building, over the single platform, its running line and run-round road has disappeared, along with the stone-built engine shed of one road which appeared to snuggle tight against it for warmth in such a place; through the shed road, the turntable was at once reached and that was poised precariously above the fast-flowing stream. The main building and platform are nowadays immaculately kept by the South Tynedale Railway Company. The Company was formed in 1976. A passenger train ran on 30 July 1983 and formal opening was by the Earl of Carlisle on 25 May 1984. Their rail gauge is 2ft, with steam traction prominent, and the course is on the first miles from Alston of the former B.R. branch line.

The Newcastle & Carlisle Railway was early on the cross-country scene and opened progressively during 1835-38. It is active today with passengers and long-range mineral traffics. At Haltwhistle, the branch line diverged from the N & C R across its South Tyne river viaduct and climbed for most of the 13 miles to Alston ; opened 17 November 1852, closed after the last train on 1 May 1976 and lifted by early 1979.

Alston station had in its time sent away minerals from such as the Vieille Montagne Company and the nearer Walton Limestone Company/Walton's Coal & Lime Co. Ltd. and products of local engineers. The number of passenger trains was increased in LNER days, 1920s and 1930s : six each way in 1938 and 1948, plus Saturday extras. During the 20th century, a NER class 0 (LNER G5) 0-4-4 Tank engine was normally based at Alston engine shed for passenger working; one could quote Nos. 1755, 1795 and 2086 (which later appeared here as 7315), also 67265 (onetime 1868) in BR times. These were supplemented each day by a six-coupled goods engine. An ingenious effort was made to achieve sensible economy by running passengers morning and evening and freight/mineral in middle-day, using a single locomotive, itself stationed at Alston. It was BR class 3 2-6-0 tender loco No. 77011, built 1954 at Swindon, which came here quite new and stayed until the little engine shed closed w.e.f. 27 September 1959. Then diesel multiple unit working took over passengers, until 1976. Provision for freight and coal at Alston ended away back, w.e.f. 6 September 1965.

Descending outwards from Alston by rail, Lambley station was reached in 8½ miles and followed by a spectacular viaduct. Just short of this structure a somewhat obscure NER branch diverged leftwards - indeed ran relatively straight ahead, for about a mile, to a spot styled 'Lambley Fell'. Restoration, at some £500,000, of Lambley viaduct (of 1852) is being tackled by the North Pennine Heritage Trust, from 1994.

The Brampton Railway

At Lambley Fell there was informal end-on access to 'The Brampton Railway'. Our perspective is aided by taking this historic line or, nowadays, its rural course, broadly eastward for a few miles. This takes in passage of Haltonleagate and Midgeholme nearly to the old-world workshops buildings and incline head at Hallbankgate. Thus, one turns aside to tramp south by the short but steep branch line (course) which attained Gairs Colliery in 1908-09 and gave it a rail outlet until 1936.

The Brampton Railway derived from waggonways of back to 1790 on Lord Carlisle's lands. As a true mineral *railway*, serving mainly His Lordship's collieries, its genesis was in 1838, concurrent effectively with the Newcastle & Carlisle Railway (which came to connect at nearby Brampton Junction). James Thompson was its progenitor and he and family successors maintained the lease and railway working until 1908. The Naworth Coal Company/Naworth Collieries/N.C.B. then in turn leased and controlled the Brampton Railway until its winding up, on the ground, in March 1953. With a history allied to the Stephenson lore of Tyneside and even ownership of ROCKET from Liverpool as its first steam locomotive, the 'Brampton' produces much to read up and explore, while the former Thompson mansion Farlam Hall, near Hallbankgate, provides hospitality for meals and accommodation.

At Gairs Colliery (1150ft), onetime railhead, on its bleak hillside, one's back may be turned to nearby Cold Fell (2039ft); then Hynam Bridge is perceived 1½ miles westward, down in Geltsdale. A major water pipeline crosses the Gelt close by Hynam Bridge and hints at sources in the river's head waters. Object of the aqueduct is a waterworks 1¼ miles further south west, including Castle Carrock reservoir itself nestling in the north Pennine beck of that name and with its delightful village a stonesthrow distant.

There is a story of 3ft gauge construction railways in Geltsdale and Castle Carrock valley. It is worth heading 10 miles more westward, to the city of Carlisle, to seek a reason, even if delving there and returning to explore these twin - and delightful - dales ends in a mystery.

At Midgeholme, Brampton Railway, 16 May 1946, locomotive STEPHENSON 0-6-0 saddle tank Andrew Barclay 1879 of 1926, with driver Finlayson of the Naworth Coal Company, has arrived from Hallbankgate incline head with 'empties' for loading at the colliery near Midgeholme.

Hallbankgate loco shed, looking eastward, with the incline head being behind the camera and giving access to Brampton Junction with the Newcastle & Carlisle line of the LNER. The gatehouse is seen (then) controlling the level crossing over the road to Alston (left at this point).

At the incline foot, the west end of Kirkhouse layout; the gasworks and workshops, with locomotive TINDALE 0-6-0 saddle tank by Avonside Engine Company 1954 of 1926, seen on 16 May 1946.

One of the Brampton Railway's noted relics; this locomotive was originally TICHBORNE 0-6-0 ST Robert Stephenson 2011 of 1872; rebuilt at Kirkhouse workshops in 1879 as 0-6-0 *tender* loco; rebuilt 1901 by Andrew Barclay with a cab; rebuilt again 1909 as 0-6-0 side tank and named BELTED WILL - and thus caught by Ken Nunn in August 1914. The loco is believed to have existed until circa 1928.

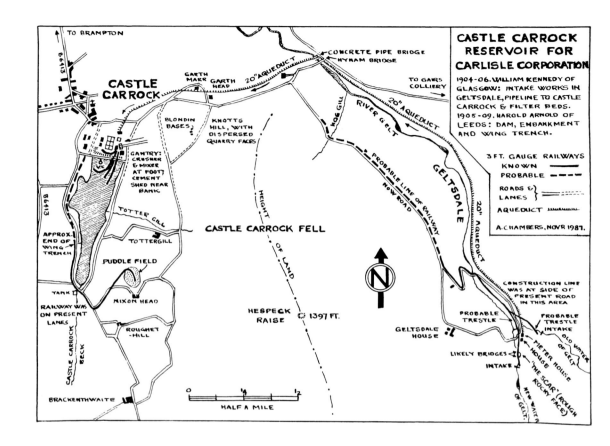

In upper Geltsdale, probably in winter 1905-06, a temporary trestle bridge takes the 3ft gauge track a little further rightwards to reach the construction weir and intake works on the New Water of Gelt. KUROKI is the locomotive Hudswell Clarke 718 of 1904 which William Kennedy Ltd provided for the railway that he put down.

Chapter Five

Geltsdale and Castle Carrock - and Carlisle

A decade of vacillations

In the 1890s, Carlisle's public water supplies left much to be desired. There was significant dependence on pumping from the river and the service reservoir at Harraby was at only 125ft o.d. In 1892, the distinguished consulting engineer James Mansergh, of London, who had been concerned as then junior partner in a report to Carlisle dated 1866, was invited to investigate anew. His principal assistant Mr Strachan and a son of James Mansergh made preliminary investigations in September 1892. The Mansergh reports of 31 January 1893 and 28 December 1893 did not feature Geltsdale/ Castle Carrock but emerged with a recommendation to draw waters from Skiddaw Forest and impound them by creating a reservoir at Mosedale; this emerges from the north east of the Skiddaw heights and the site would probably have produced a spectacular lake, in the head waters of the river Caldew. An estimated cost of £90,000 was quoted in February 1894, but no action was taken.

Mr C.B. Newton, the city of Carlisle's gas and water engineer by 1897, was called upon to look into the shortcomings of the water supplies. He favoured drawing primarily from Geltsdale, in north Pennine territory, south eastward of Carlisle. In the absence of a geologically secure site for a suitable dam in Geltsdale, Mr Newton's report of 4 May 1897 set out a relatively elaborate scheme. Impounding would be from converging mountain streams, the Old and New Waters of Gelt, and transferring the waters thus gathered by aqueduct to a reservoir to be formed in the next valley westward, above Castle Carrock village. At this point the city's water committee turned not to Mansergh but to E.M. Eaton of Westminster to consider the alternatives and advise them. Following his recommendations of September 1897, the committee advised the city council on 6 October 1897 to proceed with the Gelt/Castle Carrock scheme at an estimate of £120,000, inclusive of aqueducts to Carlisle and a service reservoir on the approaches to the city. Objections by the Earl of Carlisle in particular were negotiated upon and an Act of Parliament authorising the works was secured in 1898.

With the pump engines at Carlisle unreliable, progress was essential. Thus (December 1898) Mr Newton was to be appointed 'Engineer' for executing the Geltsdale gravitation scheme, estimated cost now £130,000, with commission to him of 2½ per cent on this figure - presumably additional to his normal salary of £500 p.a. After debate, at 20 June 1899, Edward M. Eaton, of Westminster, was appointed 'Consulting Engineer', C.B. Newton to be '(Project) Engineer' and John Campbell Boyd, of Whitehaven, 'Surveyor and Resident Engineer'.

A very detailed specification was prepared by C.B. Newton, dated March 1901, and in July 1901 tenders were secured, as follows :-

W. Grizenthwaite,	Penrith	£141,835
John Best,	Edinburgh	£131,640
P. Drake,	Bradford	£113,122

One knows these firms, of whom John Best would be the most experienced at the time, as concerns reservoir construction works. The water committee, seemingly, did not care for the prices quoted, and blamed their engineers, declining to accept that contract prices generally were rising at the time (something which accelerated in the prosperous years which followed). They promptly dismissed both Mr Eaton and Mr Newton and placed the project in abeyance. Mr Newton moved then or shortly to private engineering advisory practice; in 1907 he was at Whitehall Chambers, Carlisle and wrote 'to seek payment for his work', but was vouchsafed no reply by the Corporation.

Acquisitions of land for the proposed works continued through 1900-05, Lord Carlisle's estates being much involved. Meanwhile, reversion was made to James Mansergh & Sons, who reported in December 1902 on Carlisle's water supply as a whole. They clearly took in the entire Geltsdale/Castle Carrock scheme and visualised the need for an exceptional wing trench on the west side of Castle Carrock reservoir. They estimated £243,000 and embraced all the works onwards to Carlisle. The retention of Manserghs as the Consultant Engineers was agreed in March 1903. After the death in July 1905 of James Mansergh (1834-1905), his son Ernest L. Mansergh was prominent.

Placing of contracts

Two main contracts resulted, namely:-

Contract No.1 : June 1904 with William Kennedy Ltd., of Partick, Glasgow, tender £120,377 for the intake works in Geltsdale; the gravitation mains; filter bed works at Castle Carrock; and Cumwhinton service reservoir (the works in practice commencing in September 1904 and eventually costing £129,768.16.11d).

Contract No.2 : September 1905 with Harold Arnold & Son, of Doncaster, tender £61,733 for Castle Carrock dam and formation of reservoir; there had been 16 competitive tenders and Manserghs influenced the selection of Arnolds. (The eventual cost was £270,000 but, as will emerge, a deeper than anticipated embankment trench was necessary).

Gilkes & Company, Kendal, secured a parallel contract to instal water turbines and centrifugal pumps at Castle Carrock site. The Company is today the respected Gilbert Gilkes & Gordon Ltd., of Canal Head, Kendal, known for water turbines and other hydro-electric works.

Mr A.W. Lewis, fresh from supervising work on the vast Elan and Claerwen water scheme for Birmingham - James Mansergh's masterpiece - was appointed Resident Engineer in July 1904 and saw the works through in this capacity until 31 July 1909, when his appointment ended with commendation from the Carlisle authorities. J.C. Boyd was his assistant, right through to 31 March 1909. P.H. East also figured as an assistant.

Overall scene in Geltsdale and at Castle Carrock

The accompanying map/diagram is presented to show location of Gairs Colliery (top right) and Geltsdale intakes (bottom right), also the aqueduct's devious course to reach Castle Carrock reservoir without traversing or penetrating the heights of Castle Carrock fell and Knotts Hill outcrop - extremities effectively of the Pennines northward from the Peak District of Derbyshire.

Both principal contractors used 3ft gauge railways. Their established rail routes are delineated heavily and the less precisely defined alignments are in broken lines. Beyond and between these routes, the layouts are left to the judgment of readers and explorers.

William Kennedy Ltd., and their work, 1904-1906

In order urgently to secure an interim supply of water to Carlisle, Kennedys' work was given priority. In turn they proved prompt and workmanlike.

Kennedys laid the 20in main from the intakes in upper Geltsdale, as mapped, right round the hill to terminate in an open 'balancing tank' 20ft square and with top water level, when filled, of 586ft o.d. It is on the slopes above Castle Carrock filters. From the balancing tank the raw water (derived from Geltsdale) is piped along the hill slopes above the eastern side of the reservoir, with some fed into the midway stream and the main feed delivered into the reservoir at its head - when commissioned. From the reservoir, since its completion, water (top level 508ft) is fed via the valvetower and beneath the embankment to the slow sand filters, constructed by Kennedys. The ingenuity and economy of the overall project is seen at this point; the balancing tank serves the subsidiary purpose of providing a constant head to drive the Gilkes water turbines, in their house near the filters, and they drive centrifugal pumps for propelling the *filtered water* away up to 'Brampton tank', which is farther up the northern outcrop of Castle Carrock fell, just over a half mile north east of the filters. This is necessary in order to employ gravity for the whole of the remaining way to the city. In the latter months of 1904 and the first half of 1905, Kennedys installed six miles of 16in diameter gravitation aqueduct to Cumwhinton, building the covered service reservoir there; this, about 3½ miles short of the city centre, with top water level 275ft above it and of about 5 million gallons capacity. Concrete, steel columns and roof steelwork and cladding were called for here. A 21in diameter gravitation main was installed onwards to the city. Concurrent with new treatment plant installed from c1990, the turbine house has become something of a 'museum'.

Filter beds (by William Kennedy Ltd) - and a 'locomotive'.

The making of the seven slow sand filter beds, with provision for nine, was commenced by January 1905; the floors were of concrete. The cement derived from Johnsons of Newcastle upon Tyne, by North Eastern Railway and traction engine haulage from a local station, How Mill. A local pit supplied washed sand. Freestone for crushing and concrete making was from the quarries on Knotts Hill (more of this anon). Materials were conveyed beside the east border of the filter beds and across them in side-tipping wooden wagons on track of 3ft gauge. The machine which provided traction on the short run here was quite a contraption. It was not a crane but may have started out as a mobile upright boiler intended for use with steam pumps or tools. Its chassis was short and solid-looking, on four rail wheels, and with substantial buffer blocks flanking a central coupling hook and chain at each end. A tank, painted and lined out, was affixed on one of the short end platforms, up to about half the height of the vertical boiler. A casing at the opposite end must have taken in a steam engine unit, conceivably with pump or compressor as well as drive to the wheels, which were tucked well under the chassis. The central chimney emerged from a conical top casing of the boiler. Pipes (steam pipes?) came out from each side at the base of the chimney and drooped at each side as 'arms akimbo'. A small building hereabouts was suggestive of a loco shed. By August 1906 the seven filters were about complete and mostly filled with sand. They were eventually superseded by elaborate new water treatment plant in 1990-1993.

In Geltsdale

On 31 May 1905, Manserghs were able to report on William Kennedy Ltd. that 'the contractors' light railway is now within about 400 yards from the junction of the waters' and on 28 June 1905 'the light railway to the junction of the waters has been completed and a start made near the old water weir with the 15in collecting pipes from the Tarnmonath Springs........... At Gelt bridge concrete is in the abutment foundations and wing walls on both sides of the river are complete ..... a start made with the ashlar (namely bridge masonry).... over 500 men.... other work satisfactory.'

Part of the contemporary works with those of Kennedy: the measuring house and house for reservoir keeper in upper Geltsdale. The Old Water of Gelt flows down the north Pennine valley, through the wooded cleft. Kennedy's construction railway followed the near side of the stream and crossed it behind the tree to the left in order to join his access line (already seen) to the 'New Water', which is between the foreground walls. View of July 1980.

'Mail train in Geltsdale', worked by loco KUROKI for William Kennedy. It is believed to be near the then new Gelt bridge and about to take navvies 'upstream' to the intake works on 'Old' and 'New' Waters of Gelt.

Gelt bridge, as newly constructed over the Water of Gelt, the headwaters and intakes being up right. The steep and sinuous 3ft gauge railway ascent in the foreground is probably seen here in autumn or winter 1905. Its location and objects are debated in the text. Loco KUROKI again figures.

From the site of the new Gelt river bridge up dale to the junction of the waters is about one third of a mile and Kennedys' 3ft gauge railway was here sited east of the stream and between its banks and the present road, with the 20in main (being) laid immediately east of the railway and road. Near the junction of the 'Old and New Waters' the line divided and the respective extensions up-dale, each about 250 yards, reached almost to the weir being constructed on each tributary Water - with several trestle viaducts (see sketch map, and photographs). Concrete and masonry, including Shap granite for the sills, were imported for these weirs and intake works; hence the need for substantial railway branches to bring materials, men also being conveyed - on the 'mail train'. The making up of the road, the major bridge and the pipelaying (and a pipe bridge at Hynam) provided further work. A steam derrick crane adjoined the railhead and weir on the Old Water - and probably likewise on the New Water. The rail branch by the New Water passed 'the Scar', which may have been excavated to give the stream a clearer course downstream of the weir. No evidence has been detected of Kennedys' line continuing down the Gelt side for handling aqueduct pipes - north of where the handsome new Gelt bridge was built. As seen on our map and a contemporary illustration, the railway here swung over the new bridge (completed in August-September 1905) as soon as it was built and was then carried up the new and winding road. The railway was substantial and well ballasted and obviously adhesion worked by Kennedys' steam locomotive. The relative ferocity of the ascent can be established on foot (or by car) today. From the top of this winding ascent the road, essentially now for permanent access to and from the Geltsdale installations, takes an easier but undulating course of about $1\frac{1}{3}$ miles, by 800ft contour along the west side of Geltsdale and with fine open vistas.

Near the top of the winding hill, farm cottages were built circa 1954. A resident, Mr Bob Bowman, has recalled that until the top road, just described, was resurfaced in the late 1960s, its surface on northwards was corrugated, suggestive of indentation by railway sleepers; observe therefore the broken line on our map, The railway was evidently operating in September 1905, when Kennedys' workforce reached a peak of 700 men.

Just above the confluence of the Waters, a handsome stone house dated 1906 was erected under contract (of 8 June 1906) with builder John Heward of Brampton, whose tender had already been accepted (17 January 1906) for a broadly corresponding cottage beside Castle Carrock approach drive. At Castle Carrock a site superintendent has continued to reside but sadly the remote Geltsdale house has not been occupied in recent years; Mrs Shipman and daughter Miss Shipman have happily recalled their family residence there for 39 years, from January 1927 until 1966. A house was built at Cumwhinton, by W. Latimer, of Carlisle.

. . . .

An extra job which Kennedys took on was the laying of a branch main from the Castle Carrock-Cumwhinton aqueduct, near the Eden river, to serve Corby Castle, as agreed by the Corporation with Philip J.C. Howard away back in November 1898.

. . . .

Kennedys' workforce declined at the end of 1905 - to 200 in the period February-April 1906 and the firm was removing their plant and materials in September-October 1906. Meanwhile Arnolds were setting to work on 'Contract No.2', for Castle Carrock reservoir construction. At 4 December 1905 the Corporation received a strong complaint from Brampton Rural District Council of damage to their roads.... 'so serious.... caused by the heavy traction engines employed trailing individual loads of excessive weight, ranging frequently from 30 to 35 tons each journey.... a very thick covering of metal is required, which will need to be consolidated by steam rolling.' In response via the Corporation, Messrs Kennedy and Arnold say they have 'confined themselves to the use of the one road leading from How Mill station to Castle Carrock, via Castle Carrock village.' This would be about three miles, on by-roads in those days. No rail link from How Mill station to Castle Carrock was ever put down.

. . . .

An event of significance, which effectively rounded off Kennedys' work, took place on 16 August 1906. This was inauguration of the water supply from Geltsdale and Castle Carrock, via Cumwhinton reservoir, to the city of Carlisle, performed by Sir Benjamin Scott, chairman of the Geltsdale committee of Carlisle City Council. The benefits of the Castle Carrock reservoir itself were of course not then available.

....

Locomotive, 3ft gauge, of William Kennedy Ltd, of Glasgow, on the Geltsdale project

Apart from the 'coffeepot' (upright, boiler) contraption which has been described at the filters, only one locomotive, property of Kennedys, is known to me at the sites, namely:-

KUROKI   0-4-0 Saddle tank oc 8in x 12in
          by Hudswell Clarke 718 of 1904
          supplied new from HC's works at Leeds on 23/11/1904 to William Kennedy Ltd., Contractors, Partick, Glasgow, with name as above
          The name derived from the Russo-Japanese war of the period; General Kuroki was the victor of the battle of the Yalu, this being the first instance of an Asian army beating a European force while using comparable tactics and weapons.
          The makers despatched the loco to Carlisle station, turned out nicely painted and lined. The fitting of sprung buffers is noteworthy on a narrow gauge loco for such duties as in Geltsdale.
          I am only aware of Kennedys using it in Geltsdale and it probably left in Sept-Oct 1906, reappearing on Sir John Jackson's job in wild Kinlochleven/Blackwater, project of 1907-10.

The work of Harold Arnold & Son, at Castle Carrock, 1905-1909

Under Arnolds' regime, their workforce rose to a maximum of 190 in spring 1908 and then fell back. They erected a modest village of huts on the slope above the west end of the dam site, believed to be several office, stores or like buildings and four huts for men's accommodation, these last put up in February-March 1906. 'Navvyman' (Dick Sullivan's father) recalled that lodging here was 40 to a hut - 'but in single beds'; site practice had in general advanced by this time beyond 'double banking' where one man occupied a bed by night and another by day. The permanent house built in January 1906 would be occupied promptly by professional staff, some of whom probably also secured 'digs' in the old village, small but hospitable and with a couple of pleasant inns to this day. Edward Thompson, father of the Misses Thompson of Castle Carrock, was a butcher and supplied the navvies' camp, while their mother baked for its needs. The Corporation made a grant for attendance of a missioner under the auspices of the Navvy Mission Society.

The site of the group of quarry faces has been mentioned and figures on the map - away up eastward of the embankment site and filter beds, on Knotts Hill. It provided fine grained stone ('freestone') for concrete making. To bring down the stone, the ropeway, colloquially the blondin, was supplied by Bullivants to Arnolds. It was about 1100ft long (believed to mean 'there and back') and traversed five spans. Slight bends in the line of rope are remembered as leading to buckets toppling off. During his short sojourn at Castle Carrock 'Navvyman' 'watched the blondin to see it was going alright.... sixpence per hour just seeing the thing kept running.'. The descending stone was tipped out at the foot onto the crusher stage, and fed into the east side crusher and concrete mixer; all this plant and the ropeway were driven by a 2hp portable engine. The cement for concrete making had been brought in from How Mill station, as mentioned earlier, and also had to be delivered at the duplicate plant at the west end of the bank.

Central to Arnolds' work was as usual the formation of the dam embankment. This was not without trouble here. Excavation of the main trench took from February 1906 to February 1907 and in the intermediate winter frost and snow delayed work, with major 'slips' occurring and provision having to be made for continuous pumping from January 1906 until at least September 1907. For this purpose a shaft 10ft square was sunk on the downstream side of the trench, using three pumps and extracting at least 10,000 gallons per hour, in order to avert flooding of the trench and withdrawal of men. A costly situation arose when digging revealed a particularly troublesome spring and Manserghs had to require the excavation of the trench in part 80ft deeper than anticipated at the time of prior survey - thus reaching a maximum of 130ft below ground. Eventually, concrete was put in from March to July 1907: a tongue of concrete 6ft deep, capped by a shoe of concrete. This was no sooner done when, in July 1907, another strong spring, upstream of the trench, accentuated the flooding. A temporary circular sump was taken down through the concrete 'tongue' and to 103ft deep. Pumping, plugging and digging of silt by grab and then manually was resorted to. When the pump at this point failed for seven minutes, the water rose 20ft in the circular shaft and drove out the one man engaged in digging for whom there was room at any one time. A diver had to be employed for an aggregate of over four hours daily until the problem was overcome. Filling of the trench with puddle-clay, on top of the concrete, was begun in late summer or autumn 1907. Only when it reached ground level, at which level the trench width was 13ft tapering to 6ft at the ends, could the main pumping be terminated. This was a winter of fair weather and with continuous work the building up of the embankment reached full height and was puddle-filled to its top by the end of October 1908. Building and equipping the valve tower occupied June 1906 until about April 1908. The embankment is 1078ft long, its top height 513ft o.d.

The wing trench - greater in length at 2050ft than the main trench, was excavated in earnest from July 1907 and it was finished, filled with puddle, by 1 January 1909. It is located on the west side of the reservoir, linking with the main trench at the north west corner, and extends about two thirds of the 3000ft length of the lake - somewhat exceptional. As completed, the maximum width of the reservoir is 900ft and its capacity 180 million gallons, with top water level 508ft o.d. Arnolds constructed a stepped weir at the upper end, to carry the main entry of water from Geltsdale. They made provision for passage of the Castle

Castle Carrock reservoir. The view is westward during the works of Harold Arnold & Son, probably seen in late 1906. The filter beds, part of Kennedy's contract, are nearly finished to the right, downstream. Arnolds' major quarry area is up the hillside from which the view is seen. The gantries serve the stone crusher and east side concrete mixer. The trench excavation is timbered, as usual before filling with concrete (or clay), in order to prevent crushing. The site temporary buildings are on the far, western slopes and the edge of Castle Carrock old-world village is glimpsed to right.

Carrock beck through a concrete by-wash culvert 5-6ft diameter round the east side of the reservoir - achieved early in the job to keep the beck waters clear of site work. Another weir, the main overflow, was built at the north east corner adjoining the main embankment. The piped feed from the reservoir controlled by valves in the tower was installed in a culvert early made beneath the embankment, below the valvetower and just under the concrete shoe. Protection put in against erosion included the usual large pitching stones provided on the water face of the main embankment and filling (embanking) with pitching in especially the south east and south-west borders.

Clayfield, railway route and further handling by rail on site

A suitable clayfield - the quality has to be right - was located and exploited south east of the overall area at about 680ft o.d. Men loaded clay here into 1 cu.yd. steel Jubilee wagons which were taken by self-acting incline about 150 yards long on the 2ft gauge down to the pugging mill about 20ft lower. At the peak there were about 24 men at the clayfield and pugmill and they had a hut for weather protection. They also despatched the 3ft gauge trains of clay and, as a girl at Nixon Head farm nearby, Mrs Bowman recalls the clayfield just below their garden and the loaded steam trains crossing their approach lane.

The excavation of main and wing trenches - already described - involved lifting by steam cranes running on standard gauge tracks, carried on timber gantries parallel with the trenches. The three cranes for the wing trench achieved lifts of 25-40ft but the three for the main trench averaged 70ft lifts. After the excavation, and concreting as required, the clayfield came to production and the main route of 3ft gauge railway was put in from July 1907. and was operated intensively until January 1909.

Happily, an explicit contemporary account of the railway working over the 'main route' has survived. The engine is quoted as 'the Peckett (with 8in diameter, cylinders).' Quoting further: 'Each 'set' on the line

At probably the same date, this view is eastward, with the timbered trench in the foreground and gantries prominent. The cement shed is at its maximum size. A crusher and mixer are glimpsed to the left, with a ropeway tower up beyond them; a 'Blondin' (aerial ropeway) is bringing stone down from the quarries on the hill to the crusher. 3ft gauge loco **SWANSEA** Peckett 959 of 1902 of Arnolds is central, in mid distance.

comprised six $1\tfrac{1}{8}$th cubic yard wagons, on 3ft gauge, about 1¼ miles. Under good conditions a double journey was made every half hour by the loco, with 16 to 17 'sets', i.e. loaded trips, run per day. The run from the pugmill was to and round the head of the reservoir, then along the formation of the highway diversion to the sandpit at the end, whence it followed the upper end of the wing trench (itself some 680 yards long) to the end of the embankment. There was one backshunt on the descent from the clayfield, where the average grade was 1 in 20 and maximum 1 in 14 and sharpest curve 75ft radius. There were two backshunts near the bank when descending to trench level; here the grade descended between 1 in 20 and 1 in 40.

'On arrival of a 'set' at the trench side it was run onto a track about 20ft from and 10ft above the side of the trench - the clay was then cut into clods and these dropped by two men onto well-watered chutes - the clods glided and hurtled into the trench and smashed themselves up, thoroughly consolidating the puddle. There were twelve men emptying wagons, six at ends of chutes, four levelling up in the bottom; and one ganger.

'Clay went into the trench below ground level. When the core wall rose above the ground, the embankment was brought up level with its top [N.B. various earthfill put into the embankment included packed rubble in the latter stages to January 1907] and the puddle was tipped onto platforms beside the core wall. 9in layers of clay were trodden and punned down to about 6-8in thick. At a later stage the layers were 4½in thick [This would be in the upper part of the wall or 'core'].

'About 1000 tons of good yellow clay were found on the line of the trench under the downstream bank - taken out and stored in a heap for about 15 months - then put straight in without pugging.'

. . . .

Later in course of the works, probably in spring 1908, the valvetower at Castle Carrock is fully built and the embankment well up. The view is again eastward with crusher, eastern concrete mixer and cement shed, the last now curtailed. The upper tower of the aerial ropeway is perceived in silhouette to right of the cupola and left of the tall trees. A loco is at work - probably again the Peckett SWANSEA, rather than its Bagnall-built companion.

To permit the 'Peckett' to keep up its intensive 'merry-go-round' operation, the 3ft gauge 'Bagnall' loco with 7in cylinders, which is quoted as only able to take half the load, would probably handle the sets when at the trench side. In a photograph, the probable Bagnall appears to be handling earthfill - with tip wagons on the bank. At the same time, a steam roller is seen with its roller removed and being used manually on the bank top. A 10 tons steam roller has been reported at the site.

....

Locomotives, 3ft gauge, of Harold Arnold & Son, at Castle Carrock

SWANSEA	(with nameplates as such, visible on its tank, at the site) 0-4-0 Saddle tank oc 8in x 12in by Peckett 959 of 1902 - new in 5/1902 to Swansea Corporation, on their direct-labour construction of Cray reservoir. This was until, probably, 1905 or 1906, which accords with acquisition by Arnolds in time for use on the 'clay run' at Castle Carrock. It was afterwards used by Arnolds on their reservoir project for Leeds at Leighton in Colsterdale (see *Yorkshire Dales* at p. 57 for its history thereafter.) It has been suggested that Arnolds used SWANSEA at Embsay Moor reservoir site (*Bowland and Craven* p.59) - the works there being about 10/1904 - 9/1909 but, if so, its sojourn must have been a very short one, just before or just after that at Castle Carrock.
(unnamed)	0-4-0 Saddle tank oc 7in dia. cylinders by W.G. Bagnall : this may well reconcile with - PENWYLLT 0-4-0 Saddle tank oc 7in x 12in W.G. Bagnall 1704 of 1902 - new to Swansea Corporation at Cray in 12/1902 and still there in 10/1905 but being by 3/1906 with Arnolds. I discuss this in *Yorkshire Dales* at p.60 - which see for its later history - and suggest there that it would be Arnolds' Bagnall at Castle Carrock. Incidentally, it is the only Bagnall with Arnolds at Leighton which accords with the loco at Castle Carrock.

....

Completion of the contract works

Manserghs' formal completion certificate for Arnolds' work was presented on 28 July 1909, the period of maintenance commencing on 1 July 1909. The ceremonial 'opening' of the whole project, Geltsdale to Carlisle, was by the Mayor of the City on Thursday 22 July 1909. Later developments (filters and aqueducts) took place in (inter-alia) 1930, 1935, 1938, 1955 and 1960.

Mystery

Readers will probably have judged from our map, when associated with the sites and dates of work by (1) Kennedys and (2) Arnolds, that the problem is whether (and how) a railway link existed between Castle Carrock dam/filters sites and Geltsdale intakes. One can visualise that loads for Geltsdale *might* have been handled up the 'blondin' cableway and found a 3ft gauge railway route over the fell to near Hog Gill (see map) *but* such has not been revealed by tramping the tops and no old residents or workers have been located with recollection of a link by hilly roads, rail and/or ropeway. So, let's leave it, as penned in December 1907, that

'When, at the ending of the work
Comes forth the great event
The simple, sheer, sufficing, same
Result of money spent;
The men who do the work unthought
Are neither saint nor sage;
But men who simply do the work
For which they draw the wage....
Some of them.'

Chapter Six

By Rail to Catcleugh
The Newcastle & Gateshead Water Company in Northumberland, from the Tyne to close on the Border

The Project

One of the finest roads in Britain crosses the Border from Northumberland into (traditionally) Roxburghshire at bleak Carter Bar, 1370 feet o.d., some forty-five miles out of Newcastle upon Tyne. About three miles south of the Border this road, the A68, skirts a lake one and a half miles long - perhaps seen at its best on a still and sunny afternoon of late September. This is Catcleugh and it was created in the valley of the Rede by the Newcastle and Gateshead Water Company as a major source of supply to their territory; an earth dam was constructed at its southern end, this structure being about 710 feet above sea level at its foot and 810 feet at the top and supporting a water area of 265 acres and around 2,300 million gallons capacity.

The Rede valley works, including the lake, were covered by Acts of 1889, 1894 and 1902 and officially completed and opened on 21 June, 1904. Boring at the dam site had begun in 1889; a pipeline of over 26 miles south to Woodford Bridge (near Hallington Reservoir) was completed by 1895-96.

The project was designed and supervised by T & C Hawksley of Westminster. Thomas Hawksley, founder of the partnership, who had been the designer of Liverpool's Vyrnwy scheme in the eighteen-eighties, died in 1893. His son Charles Hawksley saw the job through and Kenneth Hawksley (son of Charles) was also present on completion. Charles G Henzell was the Water Company's Engineer and, following completion of Catcleugh, he was appointed in April 1905 as Engineer to Leeds Corporation, who were about to start on their works in Colsterdale and the adjoining valley.

The pipeline and associated tramways

Direct labour was employed by the Newcastle and Gateshead Water Company for the reservoir works but they started by placing a contract in October 1892 with Tyrie of Redheugh, Gateshead, for 'leading and laying' pipes from Catcleugh to Woodford Bridge (near Colt Crag on map thence to Wylam). The requisite pipes had already been ordered by the Water Company for delivery from July 1892 over an ensuing period of two to three years. The contractor seems to have concentrated his attention mainly on the southerly half of the route and in mid 1893 was employing 180 workers in the parish of Corsenside alone.

In September 1893 Mr Tyrie was in trouble with William Riddle of Low Loam farm (believed to be a mistaken spelling of Low Leam farm, south west of Leam Cottage, West Woodburn) for laying and using a tramway not covered by the landowner's agreement with the Water Company. The Company pointed out to Tyrie that facilities were limited to 33 feet (in breadth of temporary site ?), that immediately pipes were laid the land was to be restored and that if the tramway were retained by the contractor to obviate haulage on public roads he must negotiate this with the owners and tenants.

By February 1894 Mr Tyrie and the Water Company were of a mind to part. In return for a payment, Mr Tyrie gave up the pipelaying contract and handed over his plant to the Company in a formal meeting with the Secretary at Woodburn. Henceforward the pipes were laid by direct labour under the Hawksleys and Mr Henzell. They agreed 'to take over any claims for compensation in respect of the tramway' but 'the locomotive, being on loan, not to be included in the transfer of plant'. An intriguing mystery is the identity of the locomotive, probably 3ft. gauge, which Tyrie had on loan in 1894.

The Water Company had early appreciated the need for a railway through the country between Catcleugh and Woodford Bridge, in order to bring the pipes for laying and the cement, coal and other

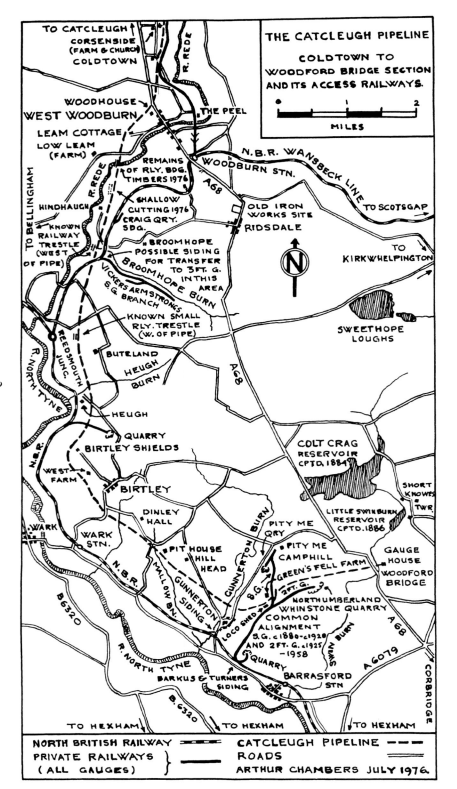

requirements of the Catcleugh site. As early as 1891 they were negotiating wayleaves for the passage of such a line with the Duke of Northumberland, of Alnwick Castle, and others. This 3ft. gauge line, to be described, followed the contour of the country with few earthworks but many major bridges and for much of its route was substantially constructed to carry steam locomotives and heavy traffic through country where winter can be severe. As seen on our maps, the main route of the Catcleugh railway gave close access to that of the pipeline from the vicinity of Coldtown (north of West Woodburn village) throughout the fourteen miles or so northwards to Catcleugh. This route has been delineated - not without difficulty but with reasonable accuracy - through study on the ground, examination of photographs and the helpful recollections of former residents or workers.

Railway working parallel with the pipeline southward from Coldtown to Woodford Bridge (about twelve miles) was probably never continuous at any one time and was more ephemeral, likely to be commenced by Tyrie as contractor around the end of 1892 and to be at an end (in the Company's pipelaying era) by 1895-96. A separate map has been drawn of this section; we have contented ourselves with showing the pipeline and main topography, including the neighbouring Wansbeck and North Tyne lines of the North British Railway, also minor industrial railways, and indicating the locations where evidence points to the existence of a narrow gauge construction railway. Proceeding southward from Coldtown, these locations include:-

1. The lands of Low Leam farm (reference in Water Company minutes, already mentioned).

2. Crossing of river Rede. The pipeline is laid beneath the considerable river but timbers in the stream imply the existence of a narrow gauge railway bridge during construction. This is tentative evidence but a river bridge would be the only means of bringing pipes northward to the Low Leam, West Woodburn, Coldtown and Corsenside sections in Tyrie's time unless deliveries were made to Woodburn station with haulage over the severely undulating A68 (Roman Dere Street) and hilly byroads, before the days of tarred macadam road surfaces. A shallow cutting has been discerned in walking the meadows south of the Rede crossing.

3. Crossing of the Broomhope burn. A photograph exists illustrating a tall trestle railway bridge over the ravine of the Broomhope burn, carrying substantial 3ft. gauge or similar track, immediately downstream of the three tall stone piers and stone abutments which carry the pipeline; unfortunately, there are now no traces of the railway viaduct and no hint of the alignment of the approach lines has been found on the ground.

4. Broomhope. The farm of this name is shown south of the point where the pipeline burrows under the Rede and indeed south of the N.B.R. - Wansbeck line. The N.B.R. knew Broomhope as the junction with ground frame for the Vickers Armstrongs branch line. In December 1892 the N.B.R. came to an arrangement with Mr W C Tyrie 'as to the construction of two sidings at Broomhope'. In March 1894 the Railway Company made an arrangement with the Newcastle and Gateshead Water Company 'for the extension of a siding at Broomhope on the same terms as apply to the sidings constructed for Mr W C Tyrie, whose arrangement with this Company has been transferred to the Water Company'. (Minutes of N.B.R. Works Committee). It is not clear on the ground precisely how the additional sidings were fitted in beside the N.B.R. line which is on a low embankment but they were obviously for delivery of cast iron pipes and, as a narrow gauge railway alongside the pipeline is illustrated both north and south of Broomhope, it appears that Tyrie would bring a narrow gauge spur alongside the standard gauge siding for exchange of traffic. It is also difficult to see how the narrow gauge viaduct over the Broomhope burn (north of Broomhope N.B.R.) and the narrow gauge towards Buteland (south of Broomhope N.B.R.) were connected. They would not cross the N.B.R. on the level; surmise is that the n.g. line could have deviated under minor bridges which pass through the embankments of the Wansbeck and Vickers railways hereabouts.

5. Near Buteland. A photograph shows a modest timber railway bridge beside a pipeline crossing of the small stream which comes down at Reedsmouth station. The picture is titled 'Reedsmouth crossing'.

6. Same general vicinity. Mr Jack Beattie, retired, of the Water Company was told of a winch near Buteland for haulage of pipes up from Reedsmouth Junction (or thereabouts); it was said that the pipes were taken southwards along their route on rail bogies, as far as Birtley Shields (about two miles), using gravity and horses.

7. Gunnerton vicinity. The Water Company agreed on 12 April 1892 to contact the N.B.R. 'regarding the use of sidings at Gunnerton' (Water Company records but a corresponding N.B.R. minute has not been found). This reference significantly ante-dates the placing of the pipeline contract with Tyrie. It could equally well refer to Gunnerton siding or Turner's sidings (see map).

8. Gunnerton-Barrasford. In the N.B.R. working timetable for 1894 'Barkus and Turner's Sidings' are shown between Gunnerton siding and Barrasford station. From these sidings a private standard gauge line climbed north eastward by Green's Fell farm to Pity Me quarry of Steel and Turner; this firm employed a 0-4-0 Saddle tank oc 11in. x 20in. locomotive, Andrew Barclay 262 of 1883, (completed by 7/1883), from its delivery in 2/1884 until the quarry closed - which was said to be pre-1914: a loco 11in x 20in by 'Barclay' figured in site auction 30/6/1916. This is believed to be the loco (becoming Beckton No. 34) which reappears at Beckton gasworks on Thameside circa 1920. Thus the Steel and Turner line would be working when the pipeline was laid in the eighteen nineties. Its route and that of the pipeline cross in the sheep pasture immediately below Green's Fell house and it must have been inviting to Tyrie to arrange for his pipes to be brought up to this point on the quarry Company's line. The 'sidings at Gunnerton' previously mentioned could well be Turner's sidings beside the N.B.R. Incidentally, the Northumberland Whinstone Company's 2ft. gauge railway, worked by three Sentinel upright-boiler steam locomotives and a diesel locomotive until 1957-58, was laid down in the mid nineteen-twenties from their top quarry by a route which took over much of the lower portion of the Steel and Turner line but the 2ft gauge terminated at a stone crusher and loading gantry on the east side of the N.B.R. (then L.N.E.R./B.R.) Turner's Sidings.

9. Woodford Bridge. The Catcleugh pipeline ended at the prominent gauge house just east of the A68 road. A photograph of timbered excavation work at Woodford Bridge (concerned with passage of pipeline under the road or river ?) shows various wooden site huts, a mason's yard and other yard areas, also two horses hauling with chains on what is presumed to be a light railway. The County Council agreed to the railway crossing the road on the level at Woodford Bridge (Water Company minute 9/10/1894).

This completes the evidence pointing to existence and extent of railways giving access to the southern portion of the pipeline.

It was reported to the Company's annual meeting in February 1895 that the pipeline (all the way from Woodford to Catcleugh) was virtually finished and that seven locomotives and two fixed engines were in use. The figures would include the Company's first four new locos delivered March-June 1894, three from Hudswell Clarke and one from Bagnalls, also three second-hand locos.

BRUCKLESS and WHITTLE (see subsequent loco list) are likely candidates and MINNIE may have been included; or WHITTLE DEAN (HC 397 of 1892), at work in the Matfen-Wylam vicinity, is a possibility. One of the stationary engines could be that at Wylam (Horsley Wood).

This locus, about two miles south west of Woodburn station is captioned 'known railway trestle, west of pipe' on our map of the pipeline as between Coldtown and Woodford Bridge. The view is looking northward and the Burn flows into the river Rede immediately left (west) of this scene. Reference is to our location '3'. Use of the railway would be by contractor Mr Tyrie for a time between 1892 and 1896, solely during installation of the pipeline.

Diversion of tramway to Woodburn Station

A Water Company minute of 28 August 1894 notes that the Company was then 'negotiating diversion of tramway from Woodburn station and abandoning the line from Broomhope to Woodburn' and by 12 March 1895 this deviation had been agreed with all landowners and highway authorities. One may suggest that the minute was poorly worded and should strictly read 'diversion of tramway *to* Woodburn station'.

With the southern portion of the pipeline largely laid and the need imminent for a heavy-duty 'main line' from a suitable railhead to Catcleugh it now became possible to build the section of the Catcleugh Railway from Coldtown fields to Woodburn station, which was situated on the N.B.R. Wansbeck branch, and use Woodburn station yard henceforward as the sole standard gauge railhead with transhipment to 3ft gauge. In August 1895 the N.B.R. gave permission to the Water Company to erect a hut and stable on a piece of ground at Woodburn and in the same year there was correspondence between the Railway and Water Companies about the provision of a siding at Woodburn for the latter's use.

Preparation for the reservoir works at Catcleugh

The virtual completion of the whole pipeline reported (above) in February 1895 is surprising as the Company had had barely a year since taking over from Mr Tyrie and it was not until May-October 1894 that all the wayleaves and easements for the main route of the Catcleugh railway from Coldtown to Catcleugh and for the parallel pipeline were finally negotiated with the landowners and highway authorities.

The Company's Act for the Catcleugh scheme in its final (enlarged) form received the Royal Assent in July 1894 and the Company resolved to proceed with the actual construction of the reservoir. Charles Hawksley however had fuller investigations to make; his final survey at site was undertaken and he recommended proceeding with the works, by direct labour, in March 1896. The estimate was £281,462, excluding buildings and land. The purchases of land were from the estates of the Duke of Northumberland. The Company proceeded as recommended.

Main route of the Catcleugh Railway

The first section of the main route of the Catcleugh railway, 3ft. gauge, started from Woodburn station yard, where traces of an incline head could be seen in 1975, near the approach road to the now closed station, itself (1993) residence of the widow of the late Mr Jefferson (last station master). 'Station Villa' is new c1992, sited in vicinity of the incline head. This self-acting incline descended northwards on a fairly straight course, single with a midway crossing loop, and terminated in a cutting and embankment (both apparent) to cross the lane by Park Cottage and immediately also to cross the river Rede and reach the meadows on the farther side. Locomotives took over at the incline foot, before the crossing of lane and river. Now there is nothing to be seen of the bridge except the moss covered stone-built retaining walls bordering the river. A heavy timber, on edge, resting on the north wall, could be seen in 1975, not readily apparent in 1993. The incline foot itself was a dangerous point, in view of the blind crossing over the lane. A brakesman/crossing keeper was on duty here and if wagons threatened to run over the road and onto the bridge he would 'sprag' their wheels. From the meadow the route was past The Peel and along the edge of its approach lane, to cross the next byroad on the level. A long and severe climb followed, trains being divided on the lands of Yellow House, and ascending beside walls up the hillside to the north, with the drove road parallel over to the west. At the top of this hillside, the line swung left (north westward), almost touching the drove road near the gates at its northern end and (still climbing steeply) soon joined the course of the pipeline in the rough pasture of Coldtown fields. Onwards, it ran on the left (west) side of the pipeline, over rough ground where its course is invisible, reaching a 'summit' close below the outlying cottage at Coldtown farm, and trains were re-formed to proceed on falling grade to cross Crow burn by a trestle bridge and then, by a major trestle, the Brig burn. The pipeline descends by syphon to pass under this steep sided valley and to climb the far side. Approaching the burn, the delightful little Corsenside church can be seen higher on the left hillside and then the large Brig farm comes into view up to the left,

Strangely enough, the Newcastle & Gateshead Water Company's wide domains were substantially framed by the routes of the North British Railway (of Edinburgh). Here is a typical passenger train of LNER days, just arrived from Morpeth, Scotsgap and Woodburn at Reedsmouth Junction (note the Railway's spelling), connecting into the Border Counties line: Riccarton - Reedsmouth - Hexham and so to Newcastle upon Tyne. A 2-4-2 tank engine of NER class A (LNER class F8), having 18in x 24in cylinders and Joy's valvegear, No.172, built 1888 at Gateshead and withdrawn in 1929, has superseded N.B.R. motive power; however, the N.B.R. carriage, distinctively musty, maintains the air of the 'NB' in all senses.

In Beeching's day, the N.B.R. lines from Morpeth succumbed totally. This is the last day, 2 October 1966, looking eastward at Woodburn station. 'The Wansbeck Piper' is being run round by loco 43063 and 43000 is sharing in the working. The animated scene was inspired by Gosforth Round Table. The small goods yard was over to left of the signal box and it was from there that the Water Company's 'main route' had for a decade at the century's turn extended all the way north to Catcleugh and close on the Scottish Border.

Back in the early Catcleugh construction days a 'steam navvy' made by Dunbar & Ruston is being delivered by goods train at Woodburn station, N.B.R.

while rightwards there are wide views across the Rede valley to the isolated farms on its east bank and, distantly northwards, to the village of Otterburn. Later, in August 1899, the Water Company decided to follow a plan submitted by Mr Henzell and lay a new line to avoid the viaduct (the minute reads 'viaducts') over the Brig but no evidence (written, verbal or by eye) has been secured to indicate that this was achieved. The levels are such that it would involve rope-inclines down to stream level or a major diversion designed to cross the Brig at a low level nearer its confluence with the Rede. Further, reliable confirmation has been secured from old residents who travelled on the Catcleugh railway that no deviation of route was made in the vicinity of the Brig burn and Corsenside chapel.

It has been established that there was an engine shed just north of the Brig viaduct. It is thought to have housed about three locomotives and was a timber building, which survived the railway by many years. Beyond here, the railway diverged westward of the pipeline to ease its gradient on the northward descent, with slight earthworks visible today, crossing the Miller burn and then the flat farmlands (and the B 6320 road), with no trace now, to reach and cross the broad river Rede within sight of Otterburn's northern outskirts.

For most of the way from this vicinity northwards to Spithopehaugh (Byrness forestry village today) the pipeline was laid under the road and the railway was on the roadside or in the meadows and woods not far from it, but with no less than eight level crossings over the main road in this distance of some ten miles. The approximate locations of these crossings are shown on our maps. The exception to close company with the road is on the 'Saffronside' section, where railway and pipeline were lower down the wooded slope towards the Rede (to left of the main road). In that area was the Currick quarry, beside the road and without rail access, used for some of the requirements of the works. The Otterburn constable complained at one time that the proximity of the locos on the roadside and their quiet approach alarmed both pedestrians and horses! Specific complaints of unprotected spots figure in a police report of inspection 26-27 March 1895 to the Chief Constable. There were a number of significant bridges in this ten miles, carrying the line over streams, usually parallel with old stone bridges for the road and new pipe bridges.

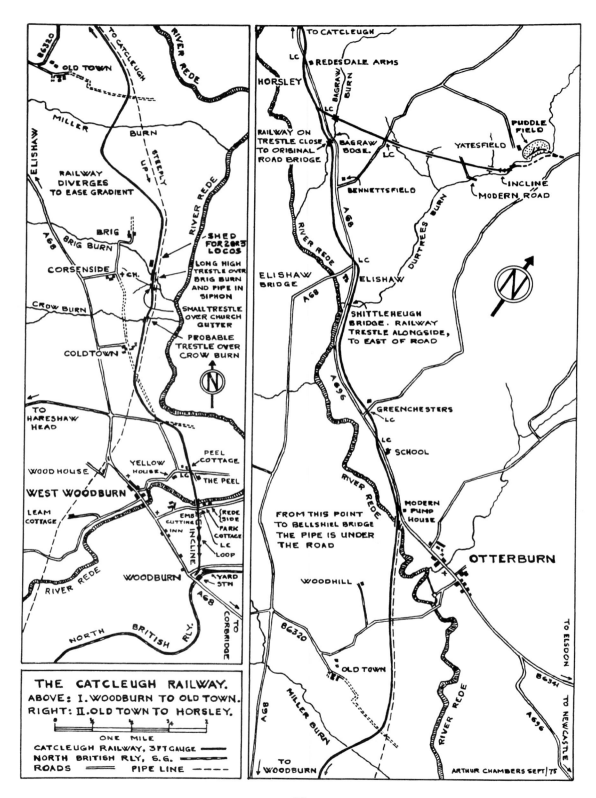

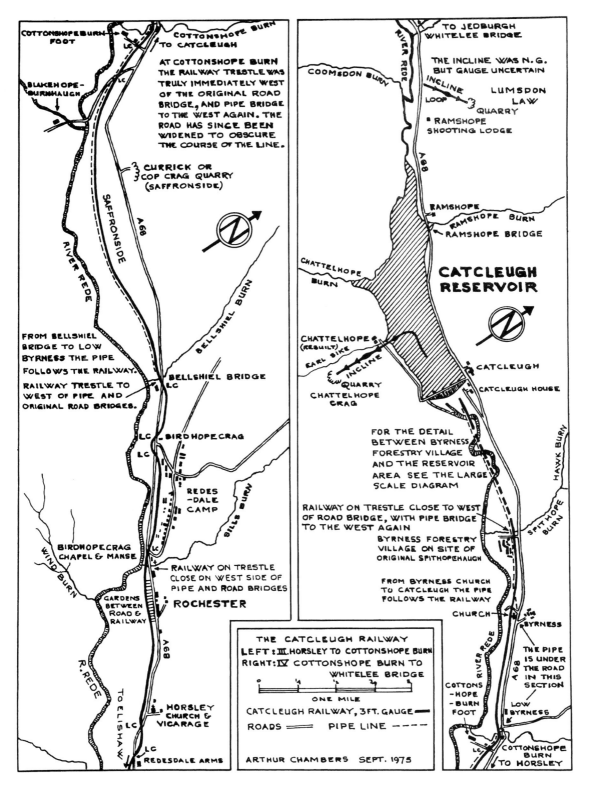

At Bagraw and Bellshiel bridges the road has latterly been realigned and this confuses observation of the railway route. The main road to Carter Bar at around 1900 could be described as a rough coach road, very much following the ups-and-downs of the country which it traversed and with constant bends. Sixty years later it was still decidedly 'informal' and certainly commanding respect after a fall of snow but by 1975 it had been vastly changed - widened, straightened and deviated too in parts, and resurfaced for 50 m p h (and more) travel. The result has been that the railway route is absorbed into the road for significant lengths. The railway in its day meandered delightfully up hill and down dale. The only villages, after the glimpse of Otterburn, are Rochester, Byrness and Byrness forestry village, the last two just off the road but the last is built virtually on the railway route. The only substantial hostelry is the Redesdale Arms, somewhat enlarged now. There are places of worship beside the route at Horsley, Burdhopecraig and Byrness.

There is a question mark over the route taken in the final mile, from Spithopehaugh (now Byrness forestry village) to the construction area below the dam. The happiest route would be to stay on the east bank of the Rede throughout, between river and road, but unfortunately the levels are all against this and one is forced to the conclusion that the pipeline was closely followed, involving four bridges over the river in about a half mile. This is the route shown tentatively on our map. Certainly the working area was approached by a bridge over the Rede and the formation is clear immediately south of the site of this bridge.

Catcleugh reservoir site and the progress of the job

The main road was diverted to a new alignment higher on the hillside than the original, leaving the old road as an access to the Company village and the working site, also to Catcleugh House, built in 1893 for occupation during the years of construction by Mr Henzell and then permanently by the caretaker of the

About two miles out by the Catcleugh route from the N.B.R. Woodburn station, Crow Burn is crossed and the Church Gutter - with Corsenside church (visible) on the higher ground to westward : **OTTERBURN** is on the lofty trestle.

Immediately north again, the Brig viaduct is by far the longest and most lofty such structure on the route. There is reference in the text. We may guess that OTTERBURN pauses again.

reservoir. The house includes a boardroom for use by officials of the Water Company. The old main road is now a leafy drive to the house and the foot of the dam. A milepost beside the old road reads 'Newcastle 41 miles' and 'Jedbro 15 miles'. Catcleugh farm was fortunate in being already sited on the hillside above the new road, and there it stands today. Chattelhope farm was demolished and rebuilt on a pleasant site above the eventual lake but on the opposite side from the road. Close by its new location a 3ft gauge self-acting incline was put in to bring stone down from Chattelhope Crag quarry. A sketch map of the 'tramway' from this quarry to link up in the valley bottom (later flooded) with the site lines has come to light in Alnwick Castle. The river was early diverted through the new tunnel (under the prospective embankment) and down the compensation water channel which was built, thus permitting the old course to be made up and creating a better working and storage area in the crowded space downstream of the embankment site. In 1898, and subsequently, cement was ordered from A Potter & Son of Willington Quay on the Tyne, coming from there by N.E.R., N.B.R., and with transhipment, by the Catcleugh railway, the standard gauge sidings at Woodburn station being extended by the N.B.R., in 1898-99. The timber built and well ventilated cement shed (see plan of dam area) was the largest and tallest building at site. Near it was the locomotive shed with two roads and various workshops were not far away. The rail layout at site naturally developed as the trench was dug and concreted, the bank built up and the puddle clay core progressively installed and consolidated. The tracks which ran through to the reservoir bed had to be given up as the bank rose above

A half mile north of Otterburn village, where the modern A68 crosses the river Rede and joins with the A696 from Newcastle upon Tyne, the Catcleugh railway route takes to following the road closely. The view here is southward, with the river to west - the railway determinedly sweeping up hill and down dale. But observe the informality of the main road from Edinburgh. No wonder the Water Company built a railway rather than attempting use of traction engines.

ground level but by that time the main demand for concrete would be over and the sand washer could be abandoned; probably the stone from Chattelhope Crag was crushed for concrete making and the tramway up to the quarry could likewise be abandoned. The demand for clay became real by the end of 1899. Access was then obtained to a clayfield near Yatesfield farm and a branch line of about two miles was built connecting the puddlefield with the main railway route a little south of the Redesdale Arms. From this time onwards the clay traffic was a mainstay of the northern part of the Catcleugh railway and four more new locomotives were ordered from Hudswell Clarke around June 1898 and delivered from Leeds to Woodburn station in October-November 1899. The material to form the embankment was dug from the reservoir bed by at least one steam navvy. A decision to purchase a second one was taken in October 1901 and one such steam excavator was used at the puddlefield. After rail access to the digging area in the bed was curtailed, the tip wagons would be hauled up the incline on the north side by the winding engine located near Catcleugh farm. It should be remembered that there was no fast-moving traffic on the main road, which in those days was bisected by the incline top lines and cable.

The title 'Bellshield Crossing' points to the bridges, railway, pipe and road, over the Bellshiel (usual spelling) burn. Realignment of the main road has since disguised the scene. The HC plate on the loco reads like 381 or 391; I deduce it is HC 397 of 1892, which was WHITTLE DEAN (see under 'Whittle Dean filters....'). The train is titled 'part of Mail', namely a portion of the 'Paddy Mail' or workmen's train.

'Saffronside Crossing' will be a little north of Bellshiel bridge. The loco is HEUGH, believed HC 419 of 1894.

Some idea of peak traffic on the railway may be obtained from figures which have survived from 1901-02. During the period 17 January 1901 to 5 June 1901 (some 4½ months) haulage on the railway (excluding the Catcleugh site) totalled 17,087 tons and the constituents were

Coal	1420 tons
Cement from Potters	840 tons
Cement from Scotts	266 tons
Granite	238 tons
Bricks	89 tons
Stone from Woodburn	267 tons
Stone from 'Quarry and Blaxter' also Brownrigg coal	2571 tons
Sand	567 tons
Puddle (clay)	10311 tons
Private parties	258 tons
Sundries	260 tons
	17087 tons

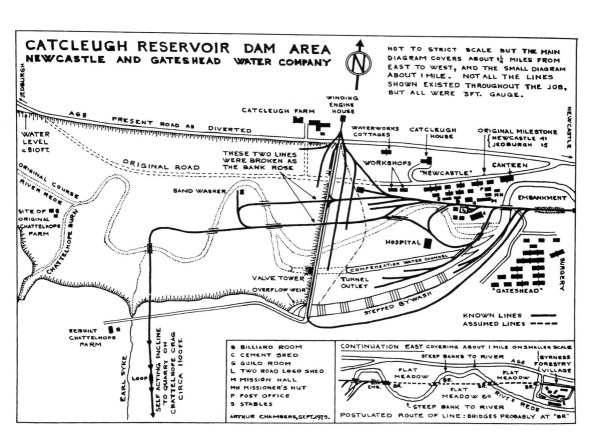

In a full year 30 January 1902 to 28 January 1903, the clay hauled amounted to 35,339 tons, from Yatesfield to Catcleugh, 'sidings' traffic (presumably all coal, cement and materials brought in via Woodburn N.B.R.) was 8,611 tons and the grand total for the year 49,166 tons. The 'tramway' costs for conveying this total were assessed at £7,014 or 3½d per ton mile. The getting (digging) and hauling of the puddle cost £2,480 or 1/4¾d per ton.

It may be no coincidence that in March 1899 the N.B.R. had arranged to replace the Tyer's train staff and ticket working between Scotsgap and Woodburn by train-tablet operation.

In December 1903 enough clay had been secured and employed at site and the agreement with the farmer at Yatesfield and those for the branch line were terminated. Traffic on the Catcleugh railway promptly fell off and in January 1904 the Northumberland County Council asked the Water Company to transport roadstone from Woodburn to Bellshiel - presumably out of Woodburn quarry, which used Manchester Ship Canal wagons and had a standard gauge incline down to the south side of the N.B.R. near Woodburn station.

The valve-closing ceremony at Catcleugh was on 21 June 1904 and the lake filled with water during the winters of 1904-05 and 1905-06, being full in January of this last year. Meanwhile, in April 1904 the Water Company gave a year's notice of ending the tramway agreements, the Catcleugh railway to cease operation by 13 May 1905. The late Jacob Robson, whose father then farmed at Byrness on Lord Redesdale's land, recalled that the last rent for the tramway course was paid to his father in May 1905. Mr Robson placed the final movements on the line in 1906.

Loco OTTERBURN reappears on the bridge at Spithope burn, a mile short of Catcleugh. The main road is beyond the railway.

Life at Catcleugh

Construction at Catcleugh does not seem to have encountered any serious engineering difficulties. There were problems with nature, often winter frost and snow; snow even in September 1898, with flooding up to rail level at the bridge on the main line, entering the site; flooding again inundating the site on 12 July 1899, 22 August 1900 and 13 September 1900. Accidents occurred. Following an accident in June 1898 causing the death of three workmen, new rules were agreed for the use of the Catcleugh railway; there is an implication that the men were travelling over the main route at the time. In May 1901 loco driver Carter was seriously injured and transported to Newcastle Infirmary. The tiny eighteenth century church at Byrness contains a unique and handsome memorial, a pair of stained-glass windows. These depict sturdy navvies at work with bucket, spade and wheelbarrow, a boy assisting or looking on and in the background a steam locomotive hauling trucks over a curving narrow gauge track. Beneath is the inscription -

'To the glory of God and in memory of those men, women and children who have died during the construction of the reservoir at Catcleugh this window and brass have been erected by their fellow workmen and friends 1903'

Deaths would be from natural causes as well as accidents. In general it was a happy time for the community at Catcleugh, living mostly in the trim hutted villages of 'Newcastle' and 'Gateshead' on opposite sides of the river. The huts were numbered up to 47, plus a few without numbers. The residential huts were single or in blocks of two or four. There was a hospital, isolated in siting; a surgery with Doctor Dodd's hut adjoining; a canteen with Mr Young's quarters; a post office, with Mr Black in residence; a billiard room; a guild room to seat 50 people; the navvy mission room to seat 260 and the hut of Mr David Smith, the missioner, also P.C. Henderson's hut. At the peak of activity, in April 1899, the resident population numbered 331 men, 79 women and 94 children, 504 in all. The usage of the Guild room gives some idea of the social life of the village.

Monday	Scripture Union
Tuesday	Night School (also shorthand class 6-0 - 7-0)
Wednesday	Evening Service and address
Thursday	Girls' social guild
Friday	Night School (also shorthand class 6-0 - 7-0)
Saturday	1.30 - 4-0 P.O. savings bank
	6-15 Choir practice
	7-0 C.E.U. prayer meeting

A school has not been identified on the site plan, so maybe the Guild room was used in the daytime as a schoolroom, but certainly the older children attended school at Byrness.

Although there was not enough daily workers' travel to call for an elaborate 'Paddy Mail' train, an informal 'Mail' with workmen on trucks is illustrated. Another picture in existence shows a 'Kiddies outing'; the loco OTTERBURN is at the head of a train of wagons with long seats for the children and another loco is in attendance in rear, possibly as a safety measure in case of any breakaway on the severe undulations and to provide banking on the steepest sections. Mrs Wylie, as a girl, lived with her family in 'Gateshead' and attended school at Byrness. She has recalled that in bad weather, if in time to secure a place in the cab, the children could travel on a locomotive. There was a tiny saloon carriage, with three windows in each side, open end balconies and four very small wheels. It was at the disposal of Mr Charles Henzell, the Company's Engineer, resident at Catcleugh House. When the loco (BRIGG on one photograph) was taking down the saloon to Woodburn, Mr Henzell would send word to the Robson family at Byrness. Mr Jacob Robson's mother travelled in this way to Woodburn and so to Newcastle and occasionally, as a small boy, he made the extremely bumpy journey with her in this 'glass carriage'. The alternative was to drive with his father to Woodburn, leaving their horse with the ostler at the 'Fox and Hounds'. They also despatched wool by the Catcleugh railway and the N.B.R. to the markets. Mrs Wylie too remembers travel in this saloon to Woodburn (riverside meadow) or on the other occasions in a 'goods train'; a permit to travel at own risk was issued for these journeys.

There was another more extempore 'saloon'; this was built on a 4-wheel wagon frame but with buffers fitted and with a glazed body and end windows flanking a central end door, after the manner of a goods brake van. Travellers by 'passenger train' had to leave the saloon or train in the meadow north of the Rede at Woodburn and walk over the river bridge and up the incline to Woodburn station.

Mr Arthur Henzell (an assistant engineer, not to be confused with Charles Henzell) lived at the prominent 'Wood House', West Woodburn and travelled most days to Catcleugh in 'the van' (this probably being the extempore saloon already mentioned), attached in rear of a goods train. He kept an eye on the condition of the way and works on the route.

Another contemporary mode of passenger travel was by the postman's gig. Mr Jack Beattie tells that in his schooldays his family lived at Ridsdale but his father was in charge of the quarry near Saffronside which supplied stone for Catcleugh and only came home at weekends. During school holidays, Jack would

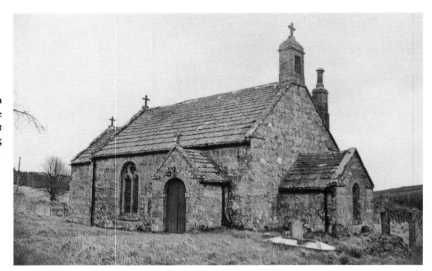

The tiny Byrness Church was close to east of the Catcleugh railway and just west of the main road; happily it survives today.

Within the diminutive structure figures a superb window, of which a major portion is here presented, depicting navvies at work on the Catcleugh project. At the bottom is inscribed TO THE GLORY OF GOD IN MEMORY OF THOSE MEN WOMEN & CHILDREN WHO HAVE DIED DURING THE CONSTRUCTION OF THE RESERVOIR AT CATCLEUGH THIS WINDOW & BRASS HAVE BEEN ERECTED BY THEIR FELLOW WORKMEN & FRIENDS

sometimes join his father and his route was with the postman in the gig leaving Woodburn station about 8-0 a.m. for Otterburn and thence in another gig which connected and took the mails as far north as Catcleugh; he would be set down at the Currick quarry, Saffronside.

Navvies who tired of Catcleugh would tramp over the Border hills to the contemporary reservoir works of Edinburgh Corporation in the Talla valley of Peeblesshire and sign on with James Young or John Best, the contractors. However, Catcleugh's roadman poet Billy Bell, writing in November 1904, quoted from wayfarers encountered:-

> I wish I'd never left the job
> I had up at the 'Cluff',
> I've been up at the Talla
> And I've been to Morcombe Bay,
> I've tried the Clyde, I've tried the Forth,
> And I've been to the Tay.
> The work was hard the pay was small
> And many a sharp rebuff,
> I only hope I'll get a job
> When I get to the 'Cluff'.

Morecambe Bay would doubtless refer to the building of Heysham Harbour for the Midland Railway during the years 1897-1904.

Locomotives on the Catcleugh Railway and reservoir works - all 3ft gauge

OTTERBURN	0-4-0 Saddle tank oc 8in x 12in by Hudswell Clarke 418 - new 4/1894 via Snowball & Co., Newcastle (makers agents). Disposed of circa 1904 to Tynemouth Corporation's Fontburn reservoir construction alongside the N.B.R. Rothbury branch and was named FONTBURN; proceeding in 1908 or 1909 to Blaxters' quarry, itself south eastwards of Otterburn - the loco was there called OTTERCOPS and ran as late as about 1947. At Catcleugh it had a 'canopy cab' only but was well boarded up.
HEUGH	0-4-0 Saddle tank oc 8in x 12in by Hudswell Clarke 419 - new 4/1894 via Snowball. Is there, one wonders, any confusion with the previous engine which is reputed to have been HEUGH when new?- but this suggestion is not supported by the makers.

An impression of Catcleugh reservoir village during its short life - indeed bleak and windswept heights appear.

Hudswell 419 left Catcleugh territory for a career with Stanton Ironworks Co. Ltd as HELEN, at Rothwell Hill, near Desborough - broken up circa 1931. Its departure was believed to be about 1898 until discovery of manuscript cost sheets for operation of the Catcleugh railway. These show that HEUGH was working at Catcleugh reservoir site in 1902. Along with OTTERBURN and CATCLEUGH it ventured little on the main line of route during that year.

CATCLEUGH
0-4-0 Saddle tank oc 8 in x 12in
by Hudswell Clarke 423 - new 6/1894 via Snowball.
It went on (as early as 1903?) to be acquired by Sir Robert McAlpine & Sons, their CARNEGIE, and they used it on construction at Culter Waterhead reservoir, south of Biggar, for Motherwell Corporation. In 1907 it passed on to Sir John Jackson for his aluminium works hydro-electric contract at Kinlochleven (Rannoch Moor), but maybe failed to survive the rigours of that job. McAlpines themselves built the electrode factory at Kinlochleven in 1908 so may conceivably have retained CATCLEUGH to play some part at that site.

BRIGG
0-4-0 Saddle tank oc 9 in x 15in
by Hudswell Clarke 504 - new 10/1899 at Woodburn station.
Following BRIGG'S Catcleugh career I have hitherto hesitated when commenting on its obscure period c 1905-11 but HC evidently handled it in 1905 and attribute the loco to George Bell, Manchester, in 7/1905; Bell had a loco of this gauge, type and make from 7/1905 to 9/1909 in the dignity of Chatsworth estate (my *Manchester and the Peak*, illustrated at p.91). Passing via the agency of London dealers Wardell & Co., it reached Leeds Corporation's Leighton reservoir (H. Arnold & Son Ltd) by 12/2/1912 (*Yorkshire Dales* p.60), then had a wartime career under oversight of the MM, from whom sold in 1919 to Abertillery Water Board (Grwyne Fawr waterworks railway into the Black Mountains). Thence BRIGG went direct in 1928 to Lehane, Mackenzie & Shand, their HESWALL at Gorple, Fernilee and Darley Dale yard (*Yorkshire Pennines* p.B126 and *Manchester and the Peak* p.58). Makers' records, and photographs, all support the name BRIGG in Lincolnshire style, whereas BRIG would have been correct for the place name on the Catcleugh route.

The surviving hut from 1895-1905, as seen in 1975 and thought now to be an embryo museum. The porch is central to its residential end and with an office portion to right. The location is just below the old main road, by-passed since circa 1895 and retained internal to the water authority estate. A stone milepost here on the old road reads
NEWCASTLE   JEDBRO
41   15
Miles   Miles

With the Catcleugh line well established, a happy scene is presented. Loco OTTERBURN, built 1894 by Hudswell Clarke for the route, is attached to wagons with longitudinal seats for the occasion, and another loco beyond - under the title 'Kiddies' outing'. The precise location is unclear.

WOODBURN   0-4-0 Saddle tank oc 9in x 15in
                by Hudswell Clarke 505 - new 10/1899 at Woodburn station.
                The problems here are to establish this engine's history *after* its career on the Catcleugh trail. An entry by its makers Hudswell Clarke records its acquisition by them, presumably for overhaul, early in 1905 and sale 9/3/1905 to Sir Robert McAlpine & Sons. They appear to have applied the name ROSEBERRY (perhaps misspelt from their Edinburgh waterworks associations) and used the loco on their Culter Waterhead reservoir contract (see also CATCLEUGH working there, *ante*), where the knowledgeable George Alliez long ago heard tell of a loco ROSEBERRY, and where the 3ft gauge operations lasted from probably 1904 until at least the autumn of 1907. In May-June 1908 Grangemouth Town Council minuted purchase direct from McAlpine of two locomotives which they had sent from McA locations to Stirling for repairs and repainting, thence to construction works on North Third reservoir, on the Bannock Burn; the plant was property of Grangemouth, although Casey & Darragh of Stirling collaborated as their contractors at North Third, as recalled to me by residents thereabouts. The works were executed in 1908-11 and the Town Council minuted both locos as sold Decr. 1911-January 1912, under names ROSEBERRY and MOUNTAINEER. John Best & Sons acquired this loco ROSEBERRY, apparently from Stirling, in 1911 (evidently end of year) and certainly employed it forthwith on their job for Bolton Corporation at Delph reservoir, name ROSEBERRY carried and makers's plate pretty clearly reading HC 505; it left Delph (Bolton) site in 1914 or after and appeared with J.F. Wake, Darlington dealer, in 1918, going thence to Ebbw

Loco **OTTERBURN** HC 418/1894, magnificently polished, is said to be at Catcleugh engine shed.

Vale Steel, Iron & Coal Company at Irthlingborough, their No.29 for a temporary construction line (authy. Mr E.S. Tonks) - and it is credible that it appeared on construction work at Burnley gas works, presumably the new works developed at Oswald Street in 1925-27.

RAMSHOPE	0-4-0 Saddle tank oc 9in x 15in

by Hudswell Clarke 506 - new 11/1899 at Woodburn station.

Like WOODBURN, this loco was seemingly disposed of early in 1905 from Catcleugh and (through the hands of Hudswells?) likewise went to McAlpines for contract work, quite likely concluding on their Lochore-Redford line (part of) construction circa April 1907-April 1908, which would suggest that it was the loco acquired at Cardenden (Fife) by Grangemouth Corporation in May-June 1908 from McAlpines. It became MOUNTAINEER either while with McAlpine or with Grangemouth and the Corporation had it with a view to the same job as WOODBURN/ROSEBERRY (HC 505 above). Its disposal was at 21/12/1911 provisionally to John Best, f.o.r. Stirling, under name MOUNTAINEER. That name applied while with Best at Delph (Bolton) from 1912 to circa 1915 (where I disallow the HC number 545 which has in the past been attributed to it). It was handled by Darlington dealer J.F. Wake, who sold it in 1916 to Stanton Ironworks Co. Ltd at Harston, in the attractive ironstone country near Belvoir Castle. Mr Eric Tonks found it with Stantons in 1944 but only 'identified' by a 'Wake' plate; however Stantons' register showed it as HC 506, presumably derived from Wake's information away back in 1916. It was seen by the writer in June 1949, sadly dispossessed of track and even shed, on the then newly abandoned Eaton Ropeway line a few miles from Harston; by then it was styled STANTON No.9.

It may be realised that there are points in post-Catcleugh history where the identities of our original WOODBURN and RAMSHOPE become enmeshed but it is thought that fact rather than surmise is emphasised above.

BYRNESS	0-4-0 Saddle tank oc 9 in x 15in

by Hudswell Clarke 507 of 11/1899 - new at Woodburn station.
Sale was in 1906 to William Benson & Son Ltd., at Fourstones Limestone Quarry, just north of the Newcastle-Carlisle railway, the loco seeing its life out there.

It is believed that all the 1899 locomotives were supplied with large permanent cabs. All the names were local to their lineside. This also applied to the following solitary loco by W.G. Bagnall Ltd, of Stafford.

OTTERBURN is now weatherworn but still clean and inspiring pride by its crew - against the Northumbrian moorland background. Let us say that this is in 1904, just before the loco departs to Fontburn, where we meet it again. In 1908-09 it makes yet another move - to Blaxters' quarry near Otterburn village, called OTTERCOPS and running to about 1947.

REDE   0-4-0 Saddle tank oc 9in x 14in
by W.G. Bagnall 1413 of 1894 - came new via Snowball.
An informant who knew her at Catcleugh believed her to be second-hand but said she was in good order; it seems doubtful if the engine did any other work before arrival - this is explained by being held in stock by the makers and completed and delivered in 2/1894, although probably built in 1892.
Probably on disposal after the Catcleugh saga, spares for the loco were ordered by J.B. Watson & Sons, machinery dealers, of Leeds. Then, an element of surmise follows. From 2/1906 (probable overhaul by Watsons) REDE may well have been the property of H. Arnold & Son and used on their Embsay Moor contract for Skipton (*Bowland and Craven pp 58-62*). If so, they released it by about 4/1908, with the Embsay Job well advanced, as in that month spares were ordered by Sir John Jackson, who was then setting into the tough assignment of the Kinlochleven (Rannoch) hydro-electric project. In 12/1909 the loco reached, probably reverted to, Arnolds, now for their Leighton contract in Yorkshire and later a wartime job at Ripon. Here, and after, I commend the illustrated analysis in my *Yorkshire Dales* at pp 58-59, which seeks to link into later history now believed to be of the same locomotive.

BRUCKLESS	0-4-0 Saddle tank oc 9½in x 14in
by Hunslet 564 of 1892
which had been new to Birmingham based dealer Joseph Buggins & Company (per makers' records) but in fact worked for T.S. Dixon, contractor, as BRUCKLESS on building the Donegal-Killibegs 3ft gauge branch line in Ireland (op. 18/5/1893) and was offered for sale in 1/1894. It is thought to have come directly to the Newcastle & Gateshead Water Company, circa 1894. The makers record it with Newcastle & Gateshead in 7/1897 and likewise in 3/1905, and a photograph in possession of a Redesdale family shows the name BRUCKLESS. A photo of a bywash at the Catcleugh site depicts a beautifully clean little Hunslet loco with tall, slender chimney, capped, likely to be this loco, and probably being the 'Hunslet' advertised 10/5/1905. Water Company records confirm that BRUCKLESS was active on their railway in 1901 and 1902 (data for other years not available).
It was acquired via J.B. Watson & Sons circa 2/1907 by Preston Corporation and used on the enlargement of Spade Mill reservoir, Longridge, with local name DILWORTH, probably there 1907-10 (*Bowland & Craven* p.18). It was then with Skye Marble Company on their Torrin - Broadford line, named SKYLARK, from 1910 or the beginning of 1911 until late 1913; then going on to work on Dublin Corporation's Vartry Upper reservoir, lying there in wartime and working in the post-war years, broken up circa 1925 on completion (this era a little amplified in *Bowland & Craven*).
MINNIE	0-4-0 Saddle tank oc 8in x 12in
by W.G. Bagnall 1426 of 1894
The makers' first entry shows this loco ordered for supply to contractor Enoch Tempest and with the family name 'Minnie', after one of Enoch's daughters. This in itself was strange, as Enoch already had a Bagnall-built 3ft gauge loco called 'Minnie', built in 1887, albeit smaller, with 6½in x 10in cylinders, and that was working on his current major contract at Clough Bottom in Lancashire (job of 1891-96) and went on to serve Tempest for some years. Presumably Enoch Tempest decided that the work was well in hand on the site and this (replacement?) more powerful loco was not required ; Bagnalls recorded an order for the loco (per agents Snowball & Company) for the Newcastle & Gateshead Water Company and it was duly delivered to them 24/2/1894 - with name MINNIE! Spares orders for the Water Company between 4/1894 and 11/1903 confirm its presence with them. In 1901-02 it was not working on the Catcleugh main route or puddle duties, but it could possibly have been confined to the main site, or just possibly used at that time at Whittle Dean, a site discussed later.
After 11/1903 it disappeared from its makers' ken and by 7/1907 it belonged to Kneeshaw Lupton & Co. Ltd, who operated quarries at Llysfaen, westward of Abergele. They parted with the loco to its makers in a part-exchange deal, dated 8/1911; with only £30 allowed, it was probably scrapped under local arrangements in North Wales. The replacement loco at the quarry was POWERFUL 0-4-OST oc 7in x 12in WGB No. 1901 of 1911; it put in many years work at the quarry.
WHITTLE	0-4-0 Tank oc 8½ in x 14in
by Black Hawthorn 588 of c.1880, onetime of Roseberry Ironstone Company, near Great Ayton, in the Cleveland hills. My evidence for this loco being on the Catcleugh job is firstly the view expressed to me by that well-known authority the late George Alliez, but also the listing by the Water Company of WHITTLE by name (no other details given) as a loco working at Catcleugh and occasionally on the main route, in 1902. I believe it to be the 'Black Hawthorn' offered for sale at Woodburn on 26/7/1904 as I disallow MOUNTAINEER and would not expect HALLINGTON. One surmises that it found no purchaser, or none but a scrap merchant.

. . . .

The loco which has been associated in reference to 'Newcastle & Gateshead' but which I discount was MOUNTAINEER 3ft gauge 0-6-0 Saddle tank by Black Hawthorn 844 of 1885, new in Baldersdale and discussed earlier on this work. As it was converted by John Scott of Darlington to standard gauge and had a probable later history in Yorkshire - and did not figure in 1901-02 data at Catcleugh - I see no reason to visualise it there.

. . . .

A sale of surplus plant was recommended by Snowball & Company and held in a field adjoining Woodburn station on 26 July 1904. Plant offered in the announcement of the sale included four 4-wheel locomotives of 3ft gauge, by Hudswell Clarke and Black Hawthorn.

A sale of 10 May 1905 was staged at Woodburn station by Atkinson & Garland, including 'locomotives built by Hudswell Clarke and Hunslet Engine Company'; this suggests that BRUCKLESS had then become surplus. Also advertised at that time were 'two passenger cars', presumably the 'saloons'.

The early reservoirs

Catcleugh was the last built and most northerly feeding the pipeline route to Tyneside.

The other lakes were successively from north to south geographically those at

    Colt Crag -construction 1879-84

    Little Swinburn - work carried out during 1879

    West Hallington - 1884-89

    East Hallington - 1869-72

followed shortly by the tunnel from Ryal to Matfen and Whittle Dean and the series of seven reservoirs, three very small, completed between 1848 and 1857.

Quarry tramways (of uncertain gauge) are depicted in our 'Colt Crag to Wylam' map.

An early locomotive 3ft gauge of the Newcastle & Gateshead Water Company

HALLINGTON   0-4-0 Saddle tank oc 8½ in x 14in
by Black Hawthorn 156 - ordered 2/8/1870 'to be delivered at Hallington via Stagshawbank and Caldwell' for construction of East Hallington reservoir, completed 1872. This route from Gateshead is by the Roman road beside the Wall (B6318) and then north by the A68, turning off through Colwell village. HALLINGTON did not figure in the 1901-02 data of locos on the Catcleugh railway of the Water Company.

Whittle Dean filters and Ryal New Tunnel and associated locomotives, all 3ft gauge

Roughly concurrent with the work in the Rede valley at Catcleugh was supplementary construction at the old-established Whittle Dean site, with which three locomotives are associated:-

WHITTLE DEAN   0-4-0 Saddle tank oc 10in x 16in
by Hudswell Clarke 397 - new 7/1892 via the agents Snowball & Company : destination when new was North Reservoir works at Whittle Dean.
Snowball (Water Company agents) offered it for sale in 10/1897 (identity virtually certain).
Subsequent owners were John Best & Sons, first recalled on their Monkstown (Cork) contract, probably about 1902-04 and then on Angram reservoir construction in the Nidd valley, circa 1906 onwards (where the loco was remembered coming as WHITTLE DEAN and was renamed ANGRAM. It was later 'No.21' on Best's Delph (Bolton) contract of circa 1908-16, and with the W.D. in 1917-18 - and associated with the name

	of Muir Macdonald in 1920 and then from 1920 'Reindeer' on the Beaufort reservoir of the Ebbw Vale Company, built by Nott Brodie & Co Ltd., circa 1918-22. It was 'Barnsley' on that Corporation's Scout Dike reservoir and ensuing works, circa 1925-36, and finally from 1936 with Richard Baillie at Ladybower dam in Derbyshire and lying there dismantled in 1938.
MATFEN	0-4-0 saddle tank oc 9in x 15in by Hudswell Clarke 596 new 9/1901 via Snowball and despatched to Font station (sic) for Newcastle and Gateshead Water Company. Later, in 1913, came into the possession of the Stanton Ironworks Co. Ltd., at Orton in Northamptonshire, as 'Kitty , and worked at several of their sites.
PONT	0-4-0 saddle tank oc 9in x 15in by Hudswell Clarke 597 new 10/1901 - despatched as the previous loco - bought back by the makers in 11/1905 and resold 2/1906 to Sir Robert McAlpine as No. 12 on the Culter Waterhead job. It continued in McAlpine service, eventually going on in 1920 to Lewis and Harris Development Company, Stornoway; reappearing as 'McAlpine 12' for the sale by McAlpine in 10/1929.

By way of postscript to the work of these engines at Whittle Dean, the '*Colliery Guardian*' reported, October 1905, the auction in a field near North Reservoir, Whittle Dean, of 3ft gauge tank locomotives (number and particulars not stated), the auctioneers being Messrs. Atkinson and Garland of Newcastle. This auction was remembered as alongside B6318 on it north side. One observes that one at least of the three locos above had found new owners before 1905.

Whittle Dean reservoirs are sited north and south of the B6318, which follows the Roman wall. The Ordnance Survey second edition 1898, as revised 1894-95, shows a 'tramway' from North Quarry and Camp (remains of) just to the north of Harlow Hill village on the Roman road referred to previously. The line skirts the reservoirs at a little distance on the east side, passes close to the filter beds, then south to Spital and the Company's pipelines, bearing east with the pipelines and leaving them to turn south through Horsley Wood to a pumping station and, apparently, a riverside layout on the north bank of the Tyne a mile upstream from Wylam bridge. A washer for sand and gravel dredged from the river was installed on the riverside. It may be presumed that the little engines disported themselves upon this 'tramway'. About the same time there would be much pipelaying as the principal water mains are dated 1892 and 1902, with a third added in 1939-40. This Whittle Dean line initially conveyed sand and gravel from the Tyne at Wylam and stone from Harlow Hill for the construction of the open sand filter beds mentioned above; a stationary engine was used from the Tyne to Horsley Wood and locomotive haulage for the remainder of the route. This filter construction was in 1890-97. The second tunnel (3 miles in length) from Matfen Hall grounds to Ryal was constructed 1901-05 and associated works carried out. The line was at that time extended from a point at the north end of Whittle Dean reservoirs in a north westerly direction by Butcher Hill to the tunnel mouth near Matfen Hall and the use of steam locomotives is recalled; these would doubtless be MATFEN and PONT (the latter a local stream name). This route has been sketched in on our map from Parliamentary plans; it is not readily located on the ground, in fact ploughing has obliterated all or most of it.

It is interesting that in December 1901 the Water Company decided to sign an agreement drawn up with the landowners involved in order to build a tramway from Whittle Dean to Ryal (i.e. to the western inlet of the new tunnel). This suggests that the line was about to be carried over the ground above the new tunnel works. The old tunnel from its Ryal entrance to Matfen has three shafts west of the Ryal-Great Whittington road, under which it passes at 'spot point' 527ft. and three more are visible east of that point. It is reputed to have thirteen in all. The new tunnel is roughly parallel and south of the old one. It has two shafts, one immediately east of the hilltop farm at Grindstone Law (a 751ft hilltop) and the other in a small plantation south west of Delight house. Both have substantial spoil heaps. The ground above the old tunnel is rough pasture reasonably level and the line could well have been built along that route, with spurs to serve the two shaft workings for the new tunnel, but no trace of railway formations hereabouts has been detected.

In November 1897 the Water Company had proposed another tramway, this one to connect the North Eastern Railway. In September 1902 there was an agreement with the N.E.R., for a siding, also one with the Duke of Northumberland. Reference was to an 'overhead tramway'.

This is reconcilable with the N.E.R's own minuted record of an agreement with the Water Company dated 12 November 1902. The siding commenced on the Newcastle and Carlisle main line 4 chains west of Wylam Junction, where the North Wylam line, having crossed its impressive bridge, rejoined the main line on the south bank of the Tyne. The N.E.R. portion of the siding was 3 chains long and the Water Company owned a further 13 chains. The alignment, towards the river on its south side, is shown on the 1921 ordnance survey map. An aerial ropeway 1800ft long and powered by an undertype portable steam engine carried primarily coal and coke across the Tyne to the Water Company's pumping station and also to a narrow gauge railhead on the north bank. It also carried cement and bricks for the new works at Whittle Dean and the new Ryal-Matfen tunnel. N.E.R. records indicate that what appears to be the same siding survived to be taken over by Wylam Sand & Gravel Co. Ltd., under agreements with the Railway dated 4.7.1914 and 26.2.1922, supplemented by a memorandum of 16.1.1923, the Company becoming Tyne Washed Sand and Gravel Co. Ltd., in 1924.

The pumping station, indicated on our map, dated from 1876 and is on a narrow site between the Ovingham-Wylam road and the north bank of the Tyne. Its purpose is to abstract water from the river and it first used a steam beam engine and driven pump; the tall beam engine house remains a 'listed' landmark in 1993. Capacity was increased by reciprocating pumps (driven by compound steam engines) installed in 1885 and 1894. Electrically driven centrifugal pumps superseded all the steam driven pumps in 1918 and this would seemingly end the Water Company's interest in the siding south of the river and the aerial ropeway for conveyance of coal. A new pumphouse (adjoining the old) with six electric pumps was brought into use in 1950 but the whole installation was stated in April 1976 to be due for replacement by new plant a short distance upstream, a project since executed.

The base of a south bank ropeway tower, the base and bent remains of an intermediate tower in the river and a lattice tower on the north bank near the Whittle Dean railway remained in 1976; the base in the river is still seen in 1993.

The initial railway incline beyond the road crossing was a short one, climbing north east into the wood, the route then reversing and proceeding to the north west extremity of the wood (this section, loco worked, being now a bridle path and easily followed). Its continuation is lost in open meadows and extensive new road works where the old Carlisle-Newcastle road and its modern successor converge. Just north of this point a section of the railway embankment remains, only to be lost in new waterworks construction approaching the Whittle Dean filters and obscured also in the meadows south and north of the B6318 'military road'. The alignments of the access line and a probable tip line are visible at Harlow Hill quarries. The final use of this railway was to the filters, conveying occasional loads of sand.

The extent of activity based on Whittle Dean in the eighteen-nineties is emphasised by the petition laid before the Water Company in 1892 by their men for a workmen's train to run morning and evening to and from North Wylam station. The N.E.R. agreed to run the train if guaranteed £10 per week and the Company Board gave their guarantee to meet any shortfall of revenue below this sum and the train was to be arranged forthwith.

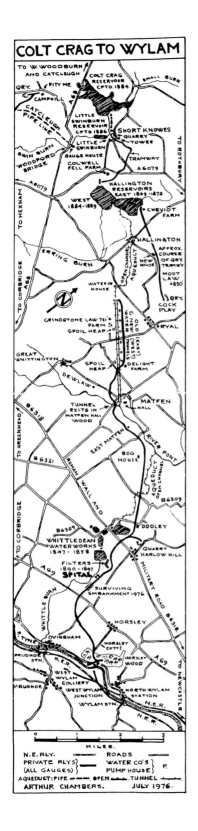

The continuation northwards of the chain of small reservoirs is taken up at Woodford Bridge and appears as 'The Catcleugh Pipeline,' map on page 86

Conclusion of the Catcleugh Saga

It has been a pleasure to reconstruct these old time light railway workings in the Northumberland hills and one may echo Billy Bell in his conclusion that

> In time to come when navvies meet
> Upon some distant job
> They'll cast their minds back o'er the years
> That time doth from us rob
> And as they there each other pledge
> In a drop of prime old stuff
> They'll talk upon the happy days
> They had up at the 'Cluff'

TYNE VALLEY SCENES

N.B.R. 43 4-4-2 tank by Yorkshire Engine Company 1913 and withdrawn 1954, later LNER C15 class, approaching Scotswood on 4.47pm Newcastle-Riccarton Junction, 16 September 1919 - probably sub-allocated from St Margarets - as seen by Ken Nunn.

N.B.R. 756, built 1899 at Cowlairs and withdrawn in 1955, class J36 to LNER and BR, on typical N.B.R. stock. The train leaves Prudhoe as the 10.0am Riccarton Junction-Newcastle, 18 June 1920, again by Ken Nunn. Again the loco is probably sub-allocated from Edinburgh St Margarets.

A pleasing scene, surviving today, here seen 9 June 1981, is at Wylam station, looking towards Prudhoe, Hexham and Carlisle. The main building is in Newcastle & Carlisle Railway architecture of the 1830s. The up platform is beyond the level crossing. One of the occasional 'overhead' signal cabins of N.E.R. origin commands all.

North Wylam, across the Tyne from the Wylam N & C station: a summer afternoon scene enjoyed by the author during a brief sojourn from Indian Railways, 19 July 1945. LNER 1795 0-4-4 tank built 1895 at Darlington and withdrawn in 1957, NER class 'O' (G5 on LNER and BR), is on a train for Newcastle, with two variants of NER stock. The line is today a footway but The National Trust maintains George Stephenson's lineside cottage on the way.

Wylam, North Wylam and the Wylam Bridge relate to the preceding Newcastle & Gateshead Water story and its maps already presented, while the N.B.R. trains to and from The Borders link with the story of Reedsmouth Junction, Woodburn, Fontburn and Rothbury, now to be developed.

Wylam Bridge, carrying the North Wylam line over the Tyne to rejoin the N & C (main) route, which is glimpsed to the left, looking towards Prudhoe, Hexham and Carlisle. Featured by Brian Reed, probably c.1922.

Chapter Seven

Fontburn for Tynemouth

The reservoir.

Fontburn reservoir is about twenty miles south east of Catcleugh or some ten miles north east of Woodburn station. It is delightfully situated. Above its head rises the high country of Rothbury Forest, providing its gathering ground. At its foot it is contained by an earth embankment across the valley of the river Font, which is crossed immediately downstream by the single track stone viaduct of twelve arches which carried the North British Railway's branch line from Scotsgap to Rothbury. This line was opened 17 October 1870 as the Northumberland Central Railway and acquired by the North British Railway by Act of July 1872. It closed to normal passenger traffic from 13 September 1952 and to all traffic from 11 November 1963. Top water level at Fontburn is 611ft o.d. and the capacity of the reservoir is 721 million gallons.

Origins.

The Newcastle and Gateshead Water Company, comparatively early in the field, impounded and piped waters in Northumberland to supply much of the county. Its Act for the Catcleugh reservoir was secured in 1894. However, it did not supply Tynemouth (which embraced also North Shields), Whitley and Monkseaton. These towns depended upon the unsatisfactory supplies of the North Shields Water Company. Eventually, by Act of 1897, Tynemouth Corporation secured authority to take over the North Shields Water Company but Parliament demanded a Bill in the next session to provide specifically for better supplies of water. Tynemouth failed to obtain priority of bulk supply from the Newcastle and Gateshead Company who however in November 1897 abandoned immediate thoughts of impounding Font waters, which had already been surveyed for them by Mr Hawksley - and Tynemouth went ahead with a project for Fontburn, recommended by Mr Mansergh, and secured an Act in August 1898. The effective takeover of the North Shields Water Company's undertaking occupied the next couple of years. By the spring of 1900 Mr Mansergh and his then colleague Mr Strachan had detailed drawings ready and on 24 April 1900 a visit was paid to the proposed site at Font by Alderman Elliot, chairman of Tynemouth Corporation's water committee, Councillor Eskdale, Mayor, and fourteen other members of the Town Council; a special train of third class saloons was arranged, also 'conveyances', which probably met the party at Ewesley station.

Contract or direct administration?

In May 1900, the only tender forthcoming for the Font works was from Kellett & Sons Limited, a west London firm engaged around that time for Birmingham Corporation. The project was readvertised and, in September 1900, there were three tenders -

Easton Gibb	£204,838. 0. 0d.
A. Kellett & Sons Ltd.	£190,945. 14.10d.
George Lawson	£164,309. 1.10d.

The pattern is familiar. The most experienced contractor quoted the highest price and the municipality, supported by consultants who must have known the relative financial and technical strengths of the contractors, placed the contract at the cheapest price. The first sod was cut in October 1901 but a year later there was general concern that the works were proceeding too slowly and accommodation for workers was insufficient, 190 men being employed by spring of 1903, when 250 were needed. In November 1903, after a final warning to Mr Lawson, Tynemouth terminated the contract, took over the plant and proceeded by direct labour, under their resident engineer and the oversight of James Mansergh & Sons.

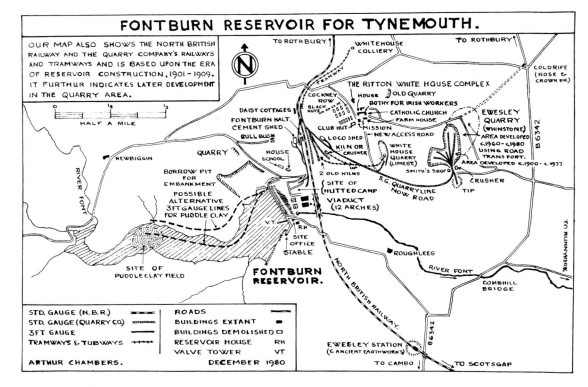

Lands and village.

The lands for the works were acquired by the Tynemouth Corporation from the Duke of Northumberland (agent: Mr Tomlinson), Mr Orde of Nunnykirk and Sir George Otto Trevelyan of Wallington Hall (whose agent was Mr J.W. Clarke). Sir George, who had newly retired from public life as a statesman, was nephew of Lord Macaulay and noted as author of 'The Life and Letters of Lord Macaulay'. His third son was George Macaulay Trevelyan (later, O.M.), the historian.

Tynemouth Corporation's village at Fontburn, in wintertime!

A broad northward view of the village, including a permanent house, locomotive shed (with two 3ft gauge locos and saloon), and filters in right foreground. This is a relatively late view, as witness the dam embankment (left).

In April 1901, Mr George Lawson negotiated with the Duke's agent for a site on which to erect a temporary village of huts. It was on the northern hillside at Fontburn - see map. The somewhat nondescript houses which lined Main Street on both sides appear to have formed the nucleus of the village. When the Corporation took over in 1903 they found the huts in a disgraceful state and promptly scrapped the wooden bunks and substituted bedsteads, which would in those days be of iron. The Corporation had a canteen built, at the end of the village near the North British Railway, and its licensing and running proved to be a recurring preoccupation and at times a source of anxiety. The building itself stood until about 1951. The Reverend C.E. Blackett-Ord, Rector of Rothbury 1901-18, wrote suggesting a navvy mission and so did Mr Ockford, secretary of the Navvy Mission Society. It was originally left to the Society to build the mission hall but the Corporation seem eventually to have built it and they contributed £50 annually towards the missioner's salary, making the payments quarterly via the Reverend Blackett-Ord; the mission would serve also as the hall, use of which for social occasions has been recalled. A cottage (hut) was put up for the canteen keeper and one for the county policeman seconded to Fontburn; P.C. George Lee was appointed 19 November 1902 and put up at Rough Lees (sic) farm hut P.C. Taylor took over from June 1903 and occupied the newly completed cottage.

Sir George Trevelyan urged on the Mayor of Tynemouth the need for a school at Font. A site was selected on the hillside 'alongside the inspector's house and behind the No.1 valveman's cottage'; these huts are identifiable on photographs. The school stood prominently on the north hillside, above the village but not so high as Bull Bush farm. The Duke of Northumberland undertook to build the school and it was a structure of pleasing appearance, with its end gables 'half timbered' above a large window. It was not fully equipped and opened until January 1905. It was divided into two main rooms; the infants and their mistress occupied one room, while the headmaster and an assistant master and their classes shared the other. The head's house adjoined and the lavatories too were outside the main building. Children walked to school from as far as Spy Law, below Simonside hill. They were allowed to set off early for home on dark evenings. The building continued as a school until 1929 and for many years Miss McKenna was the mistress in charge of the younger children. After 1929, the building served as a village hall until demolished in the early nineteen-fifties.

A shop was established under Corporation arrangements, with Post Office savings bank from May 1905, and the keepers were Mr and Mrs Pattison.

In order to increase accommodation to 250 men, more huts were planned in November 1903 and another four put in hand in May 1905. The front row of huts in the village were amongst the additions under direct municipal administration. The eventual total accommodation is on record as 48 occupied huts, although it is difficult to reach this total on photographs. The village population reached about 450, including some 250 employed men. Mrs Margaret Mellon at the age of ninety-one, has recalled in conversation that, in fairly early days of the Job, when she was a young woman, the family lived for a year or two in a hut with two rooms - thus evidently her father qualified for a family bungalow. The fireplace heated water, which was drawn off from a tap into baths or pails, as required. Lighting was by oil lamps and the quarters were cosy notwithstanding the exposed situation. Milk came from Roughlees farm, carried in pails by a donkey cart. The larger huts were in the dormitory style which was then and for long familiar on constructional sites, with quarters incorporated for a hut keeper and family. It is interesting that some of the 'temporary' houses in the village survived, occupied, until the construction during the post-1945 era of a few permanent houses for staff, in the same general area north of the filter beds and fairly well up the hillside.

The railway connection at Fontburn.

A single standard gauge railway siding was put in by the N.B.R., at the instance of the contractor, and completed in February 1902, seemingly as property of the Railway Company. Additional siding accommodation, costing about £370, was planned by Mr Mansergh and agreed by the N.B.R. and the Corporation in January 1904. This access line came off the N.B.R., trailing for trains to Rothbury, just about where the line to Whitehouse lime works and Ewesley quarry also trailed in, but on the opposite side

The village is to the left, with loco **TATTOO (by Kerr Stuart, 1904).** The N.B.R. heads north to Fontburn Halt (visible) and onwards to Rothbury. The large building in middle distance will be the cement shed, with access by both standard and narrow gauge railways.

Southward of the previous scene the N.B.R. crosses its handsome viaduct of 12 arches, delicately veiled by a drift of smoke from the site works. TATTOO is presumed to be hauling clay, well up to the bank top level, passing a permanent house.

of the main line railway. The pair of typical N.B.R. single storey cottages, in stone, which have survived the Railway, were just north of this junction and already existed at the opening of the twentieth century; they became known as Daisy Cottages. The Fontburn halt or station platform for passengers was an addition in the era of the reservoir and the passenger carrying function of the N.B.R., is discussed later.

The exchange arrangements from standard gauge to the site gauge of 3ft essentially consisted of a narrow gauge track coming alongside the standard gauge one, behind the platform of the passenger halt. Cement was brought in by rail, supplied by Addison Potter & Company of Newcastle upon Tyne and by Otto Trechmann Limited of West Hartlepool. The cement storage sheds were in the yard area immediately adjoining the standard gauge and the bags would be discharged into store without transhipment and then be available for conveyance on the narrow gauge to the concrete mixers, access to which is shown on our map and which are also illustrated. Whinstone, already crushed to provide aggregate for concrete making, was shunted across from the Ewesley Quarry Company's branch line to the exchange sidings just described, on the Corporation's property, and this aggregate was necessarily transhipped to narrow gauge for delivery to the mixers. Stone was also obtained from a quarry on the Duke's land adjoining the borrow pit for embankment fill. Sand too was imported, and transhipped. Stone required in the later stages of the project for pitching the embankment is said to have come from Blaxters Limited, where the quarry was revived in 1905 and from about 1908 had a private 3ft gauge railway beside the Newcastle-Carter Bar road to Knowesgate station on the N.B.R. Reedsmouth Junction-Scotsgap section (the Wansbeck Valley Railway). Coal for locomotives, cranes and other purposes was invoiced from several sources including the old-established collieries at Plashetts, connected to the North Tyne line. The N.B.R. probably quoted rates designed to encourage deliveries from sources connected to their system. Coal for use in the huts was being supplied in 1906 by Messrs. McKelviehead.

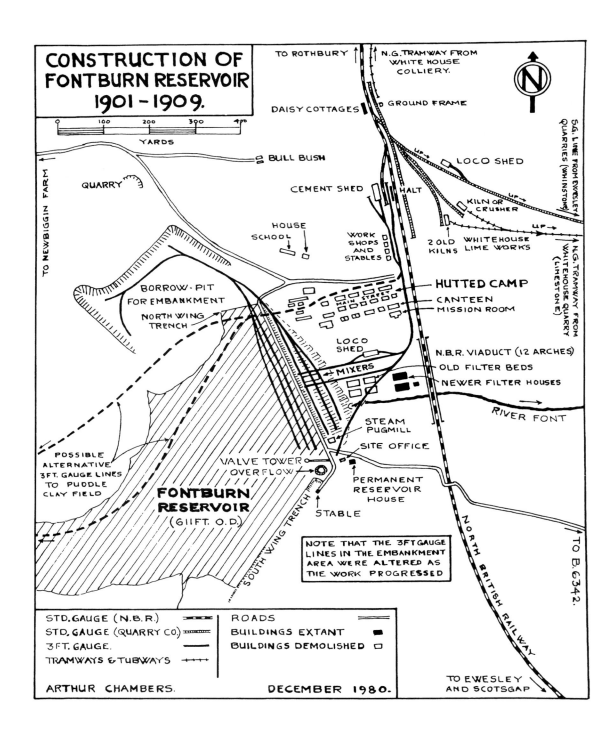

Railways and operation on the site.

A fair idea of the 3ft gauge railway layout around the site at Fontburn is given on the map; there were the inevitable changes of layout as work progressed, more especially as the embankment was formed. The main cut-off trench across the valley was 1040ft long, with maximum depth 101ft below ground and the embankment was 94ft above ground at maximum. The trench was filled with concrete up to about ground level, forming a shoe on which the puddled clay core of the dam was based. A north wing trench extended for 300ft length, filled wholly with puddle clay, and the south wing trench, partly concrete and partly puddle, was no less than 1000ft long. It was supplemented by an arm trench of 500 ft, practically at right angles to the main trench.

Supplemented by photographic evidence, there exists an excellent paper by Mr Francis Hull, the Tynemouth Corporation's resident engineer at Fontburn, whose responsibilities widened when the contractor was dismissed and who had charge until his resignation in June 1907 in order to go to the Ambergate project of the Derwent Valley Water Board - his assistant Mr H G Coventry then taking over. Mr Hull's paper confirms that all the spoil excavated from the trench was lifted by the 3 tons capacity steam cranes running on standard gauge tracks on the gantries which paralleled the main trench on its upstream side; six cranes were engaged on this trench excavation.

The receipt at site of cement, sand and crushed whinstone has been mentioned. These materials and also 'freestone', crushed at site, were transported to the upper platform of the concrete mixers in wooden side-tipping wagons of 3 cu yds capacity, by the 3ft gauge railway. The mixers discharged concrete into

In June 1904, the Corporation have taken over and set to work in earnest; TATTOO is on the embankment and the concrete mixer stage is seen.

In August 1904, this view will be north west, over the embankment trench, concrete mixers to right and loco TATTOO with wagons for charging the concrete plant.

crane skips, half cu yd capacity, and these were loaded two to a bogie, which ran to the steam cranes and these cranes placed the concrete. However, as the concrete in the trench approached ground level steel side-tipping wagons of half cu yd capacity were used and these were tipped directly into the trench from temporary track alongside. All placing of concrete in the trench was effected between February 1904 and November 1905, apart from work in the arm trench.

The clay was dug out of an area in the reservoir bed about three quarters of a mile upstream of the embankment, the considerable stone content being laboriously picked out and used for beaching the lower slope of the embankment. The clay was brought out by half cu yd steel side-tipping wagons on light track and these wagons were tipped at the hopper of the pug mill, which was driven by a steam portable engine and located in a shed alongside the embankment. The pugged clay was discharged into the timber side-tipping wagons of 1½ cu yd for haulage to the tracks abutting on the trench - haulage becoming more onerous as the embankment rose and probably facilitated by the inclined plane which ascended from near the pugmill to the vicinity of the (south side) reservoir house. The pugged clay (puddle) was spread in layers about 9in thick, each being 'heeled' or trodden in by the men on this work until reduced to 6in thick. The surface was moistened, but protected if frost should occur.

Under license from the Duke, most of the fill to form the embankment was excavated from a borrow pit above top water level, not far upstream of the bank's north end. Excavation from the filter beds and spoil from the clayfield were also tipped on the bank. Two steam navvies worked in the borrow pit, one by Ruston weighing 36 tons and one by Whitaker weighing 23 tons. Loading was into 1½ cu yds wooden side-tipping wagons, shunted at each navvy by two horses and made up into trains of ten wagons and hauled by

Looking southward across the embankment in September 1904, the concrete shoe is well advanced. An inclined railway ascends to near the reservoir keeper's permanent house.

steam locomotives on the 3 ft gauge. Eight of these train sets were in use during forming of the bank but one locomotive and crew sufficed for serving each navvy. The six parallel roads on the bank top were reached by a self-acting incline at the north end of each road; the inclines were about 1 in 6, with wheel 8ft 6in diameter, braked. Two horses were employed hauling the wagons of fill on the embankment and the wagons were tipped and the material spread by the men of the embankment gang. Consolidation of the bank at Fontburn was by a special steam roller with nameplates 'Incubu' having a smooth front wheel and grooved back wheel (roller) 40 in wide, weight complete 6 tons. Rails on the site varied from 35 to 42 pounds per yard, spiked to sleepers. The outlet tunnel, 15 ft internal diameter after lining with cast iron segments and 634 ft long, was constructed early on and completed by George Lawson, the contractor, the water of the river Font being diverted through it on 23 July 1903. The tunnel eventually carried the main draw-off pipes and also a 21in diameter pipe for the overflow from the bottom of the waste water pit to the river channel downstream. The valve tower was built above the tunnel. Draw-off pipes were installed at 5 ft, 17 ft, 29 ft, 41 ft, 52 ft and 69 ft below top water level and the first four were connected to an 18 in diameter vertical pipe passing down the tower, while the two lower ones were more indirectly connected to the 18 in pipe.

Motive power - equestrian and steam..

The site employed a considerable number of horses and Mr Laurence Perkins, son of the walking ganger and a schoolboy at Font, in later years (at Ewden) recalled it as one where three-wheel dobbin carts with hand steersmen were used extensively. Mr Hull noted that sixteen horses were usually at work, with stabling for nineteen. All horses were of course named, for example 'Birdie', 'Billie' and 'Jimmy', and they appear also to have been numbered, e.g. 'Birdie' was horse No.3. Horses and traps were provided for the engineers. Mr Hull mentions the locomotive shed as accommodating three locomotives but he

At Fontburn, additional to four steam locomotives, horses figure prominently. Here, the trusting driver surveys to rear.

INCUBU, with nameplate as such, is the steam roller at Fontburn site.

Mixed motive power takes in loco **FONTBURN**, 1894 by Hudswell Clarke; a later reference will be noted.

A Ruston steam navvy in August 1905, presumably in the borrow pit, digging out 'fill' material for the body of the embankment. Note that a faithful nag provides the rail motive power.

does not mention how many locomotives were employed at site. Four are known to the writer and it is believed that this was the maximum complement. The first reference traced to the need for a loco was in February 1904, soon after the Corporation's takeover. All seem to have come after the period of the contractor's work and their main particulars follow. It is significant that the loco shed does not appear on the 1904 views but is seen in 1905, sited just in front of the village houses. One notes, from Mr Hull, that during much of the work two locos were fully engaged in handling trains of 'fill' from the steam navvies to the top of the inclines which descended onto the bank. When a loco on this duty required two months off for repairs (December 1905), horses had to be substituted, with consequent delay to the work and this came shortly after six weeks spent repairing the Whitaker navvy. One loco would be needed throughout the progress of the works for loads from the exchange sidings and cement store to various parts of the site, especially to the concrete mixers in 1904 and 1905. A saloon carriage, on 3 ft gauge, figures in a photograph. Many of the timber side-tipping wagons carried letters 'T C' (Tynemouth Corporation) and numbers.

A 3 tons capacity steam loco crane; the view is in July 1904 towards the incline on the valley's south side, with the keeper's permanent house above.

The running of the job

It is noted that, in the administration at site, typewriters were used, with copy correspondence filed, there being no ledgers or letter books. A card index of costs was maintained. The resident engineer had two assistant engineers, H.G. Coventry and A.T. East, a secretary, cashier, timekeeper, storekeeper, village inspector, cement tester, two office boys, two staff men and two inspectors, also workshop foremen.

Each gang of men was under the charge of a ganger, responsible to the walking ganger; the latter, Thomas Robert Perkins, was a respected figure and recipient of a testimonial of esteem from his gangers and workmen on completion of the job. In the earlier stages, Mr James Mansergh tended to recommend people known to him through Birmingham Corporation's Elan and Claerwen and associated works, then nearing completion. James Mansergh died in May 1905, his two sons continuing the partnership and providing consultancy services to Tynemouth. Of interest at this date (May 1905) were purchases made on a visit to Catcleugh site, then closing down.

Incidents.

A flood in November 1905 has been recorded, as have two fatal accidents, both associated with railway working. On 29 June 1905, Thomas Bergen was accidentally run over by a locomotive and died. John Lane was fatally injured whilst coupling wagons on 11 September 1907.

The canteen was a source of problems. The contractor, George Lawson, at one stage installed his son to run it and after the Corporation took over the site, including the canteen, George Lawson retook possession of the canteen (January 1904) with a view once again to subletting to the son, but this was not tolerated. In March 1905 the canteen barman was dismissed by the borough accountant and James W. Hammill of North Shields was engaged in his stead.

The Institution of Civil Engineers held a summer meeting visit on 21 September 1905 and a party of visitors received at site in June 1907 was 500-600 strong.

The social life was helped by the mission hall and the interest of the resident missioner. The Navvy Mission Society saw to it that the children had a party at Christmas time.

The aqueduct.

An 18 in diameter supply pipe, a gravitation main, was laid throughout from the measuring house at site to Moorhouses service reservoir, Tynemouth. The laying was under two contracts, namely -

Contract No.3.   Font to Stannington.
                 Carried out by Robert Hudson & Sons, begun around July 1902 and finished soon after March 1905.
                 Hudsons had also reconstructed Moorhouses reservoir.
Contract No.4.   Stannington to Moorhouses. W. & J. Lant, circa April 1904 - September 1905.

End of the job.

The main rundown of activity was in 1907-08, with various sales of plant by private treaty around September 1907. By March 1908 about ninety men remained and on 4 March 1908 filling with water commenced, the first water passing to Tynemouth in April 1908.

In September 1908 there was still a fair amount of inwards traffic by rail on the standard gauge but this virtually ended in October with the works essentially complete. On 16 October 1908 the lake was full and overflowing for the first time. In December it was agreed to sell all surplus plant.

March 1909 was the date of appointment of the four members of permanent staff, initially Messrs. D. Munroe (in charge), D. McNamara, W. Appleby and W. Low. The official Council inspection was on 8 September 1909. The plaque on the valvetower however carries the date 1908, which corresponds with completion of an attractive and workmanlike project.

TATTOO 0-4-2 saddle tank with 7in x 12in cylinders gave its name to a fresh design by the makers Kerr Stuart. It is clearly almost new in this May 1904 view at Fontburn site.
Its plate reads
**KERR STUART & Co Ltd
852
LONDON & STOKE**

Locomotives of Tynemouth Corporation at Fontburn: all 3ft gauge.

TATTOO   0-4-2 Saddle tank oc 7in x 12in
                 by Kerr Stuart 852 of 1904 - new to Tynemouth Corporation, its identity being confirmed by the number 852 on the plates, at Fontburn. In service by 5/1904.
                 Sold on completion to John Best & Sons Ltd., used by them at Delph reservoir, Bolton. The sale to Best was circa 1909-10; date 3/1910 and price of £170 have been quoted.   It was again on the market in 8/1919.
                 The name was painted on the tank.

TYNEMOUTH   0-4-0 Saddle tank oc 7in x 10in
                 by Hunslet 759 of 1901 - had been new from the makers in Leeds 1/11/1901 to Douglas Corporation and used on the West Baldwin reservoir contract, with nameplates ARDWHALLIN. It was purchased from Douglas by Tynemouth and shipped from Douglas on 20/5/1905, the makers at that time supplying nameplates TYNEMOUTH. Sold on completion to John Best & Sons Ltd., at Delph, Bolton, retaining its name. Sale has been quoted as 3/1909 and price £170. Again on market 8/1919. Mr L.R. Perkins recalled that when working at Fontburn it carried on the chimney three brass legs of Man, as an emblem.

TYNEMOUTH 7in x 10in cylinders by Hunslet 1901 is seen in *July 1905*. Its nameplates were made in May 1905 when Tynemouth Corporation acquired it from Douglas Corporation in the Isle of Man, whose **ARDWHALLIN** it had been.

FONTBURN		0-4-0 Saddle tank oc 8in x 12in by Hudswell Clarke 418 of 1894 - acquired from Newcastle & Gateshead Water Company, Catcleugh site, in circa 1904; it had been their OTTERBURN. The makers' number and date have been checked on a picture taken at Fontburn in 7/1905. The name was painted on the tank. Sold on completion, in 1908 or 1909, to Blaxters Ltd., at their quarry near Knowesgate, becoming OTTERCOPS.
REDE		0-4-0 Saddle tank oc 9in x 14in by W.G. Bagnall 1413 of 1894 - acquired from the Catcleugh site, retaining its Newcastle & Gateshead Water Company name. Spares were ordered in 1906 in the name of J.B. Watson & Sons and in 4/1908 by Sir John Jackson; maybe at the first date Watsons were acting as agents for Tynemouth Corporation. The later date implies disposal at that time to Jacksons, who were urgently bringing together a motley collection of second-hand 3 ft gauge locos for use at the British Aluminium Company's hydro electric reservoir on Rannoch moor, above Kinlochleven. In 12/1909 it reached H. Arnold & Son for their Leighton contract, followed by a wartime job at Ripon. Actual building date was probably 1892. Mr Perkins recalled this loco by name at Fontburn and believed that it had come from Catcleugh and that it was later at Masham (which tallies with Leighton reservoir). A career in the 1920s is discussed at page 59 in *Yorkshire Dales*.

The 'Ritton White House' complex in September 1980; the farmhouse, once being the quarry manager's house, is prominent in the foreground. The silhouette of Simonside provides an attractive background.

The Ewesley Lime Works and Quarries and Ritton White House.

Ritton White House, still standing on the hill slopes overlooking Daisy cottages and the course of the North British Railway at Fontburn, cannot be overlooked in recounting the tale of Fontburn reservoir, its railways, traffic and people; indeed it deserves attention in its own right.

Two miles to the south east of the White House is Nunnykirk, where the Hall was erected in the late eighteenth century and improved architecturally by Dobson. The Nunnykirk estate appears in a directory of 1881 as 1110 acres in extent and owned by William Orde. (In later years, Colonel Orde of Nunnykirk was a governor of Fontburn school). In those parts the term 'township' was used for component parts of a parish and in 1881 Ewesley township took in Ewesley N.B.R. station and 19 inhabitants, its acreage was 932 and it was William Orde's property - evidently representing the major portion of his estate. The 'township' of Ritton White House belonged to the Trevelyan family but by 1887 it had been sold (recently) and the indications are that it had passed to William Orde. In 1887 Thomas Charlton, a farmer, occupied the White House, probably as a tenant of Mr Orde. At the same date, Francis and William Armstrong figured as lime manufacturers and stone merchants of White House Lime Works. It is understood by Mr E.G. Rutherford, of Rothbury, that the Armstrongs were residents of Whitley Bay and also had Scots partners in their enterprise. The works passed to the Ewesley Quarry Company and this Company leased the White House itself and its territory from the Orde family. At one time there was also a little coal getting activity. The lime kilns were close to the N.B.R. line, as shown on our map, and the course of the branch to reach them from the N.B.R. is visible today, along with the remains of the kilns; these last were in use

Ewesley Quarry Company's standard gauge locomotive EWESLEY No.2 by Hawthorn Leslie 1901 is at Fontburn, with Mr Smith, quarry manager, the tall figure on the right. The quarry line linked into the N.B.R. just to the north of Fontburn Halt.

until, probably, 1914 and they reopened for a time in the nineteen-twenties before final abandonment. The limestone quarry which supplied the kilns was itself not far beyond them, no more than a half mile from the N.B.R. The private branch line extending this distance and stopping short of the lane from the ford to the White House appears on the Ordnance Survey as revised 1895, but it may be suspected that the line was-then on narrow gauge, probably with horse haulage. By the time of the reservoir construction works, this was a standard gauge line and had been extended across the lane to permit opening up of a whinstone quarry for obtaining harder stone; it was from this quarry that crushed stone was brought by the private locomotives of the Quarry Company to the waterworks siding for transhipment there to narrow gauge and use in concrete making.

In 1977, only the whinstone quarry, much developed, was still being exploited - by the ubiquitous Thomas Tilling Group. During much of the era of Ewesley Quarry Company, William Rutherford, father of E.G. Rutherford, was in charge of its day to day operations. A locally well-known locomotive driver here was George Nesbitt. Bull Bush comprised a pair of houses; he and his wife lived in one until his death circa 1950 and William Rutherford occupied the other one. Mrs Rutherford has recalled that a spring behind the houses never failed to provide water for the residents of Bull Bush. Railway working to the quarry was run down in 1935-37 and abandoned around 1937 but operation of the quarry, with road haulage, was still under Ewesley Quarry Company control until at least the early 1950s.

Locomotives, all standard gauge, were employed by the Ewesley Quarry Company:

EWESLEY No.1   0-4-0 Saddle tank oc 9in x 14in
by Manning Wardle 495 of 1874.
This tiny loco, with wheels only 2ft 9 in diameter, had been supplied new by Manning Wardle to Strafford Colliery Co. Ltd, near Barnsley; they disposed of it in 1898 to Hudswell Clarke of Leeds. HC overhauled it, then placing it on at least two successive hire assignments between 3/1899 and 8/1900. HC sold eventually to R.H. Longbotham & Co., of Wakefield, engineers and machinery merchants, for £420, probable date 15/10/1900. My authority for identifying this MW loco with EWESLEY No.1 is that MW (the makers) endorsed their records to show the Quarry Company as an owner of it in later life. I favour the view that the Company set up their standard gauge line around 1900, with this as their first loco. This 'No.1' was recalled vaguely to me as a possible Hawthorn Leslie product (which I discount) and stated to be broken up on the Quarry Company's site before 1937.

EWESLEY No.2	0-4-0 Saddle tank oc 12in x 18in by Hawthorn Leslie 2496 of 1901 - came new. Sold on closing of the quarry railway, passing through the hands of Steel & Company, of Crown Works, Sunderland, and thence in circa 1938-39 reaching Sir Hedworth Williamson's Limeworks, Fulwell, Sunderland, their NICHOLAS.
EWESLEY No.3	0-4-0 Saddle tank oc 10in x 18in by Andrew Barclay 1250 of 1911 - came new. Lay in a siding at site, awaiting disposal, in 1938, and for a long time before going for scrap.

At 1 November 1902, the North British Railway did *not* show a private siding for Ewesley Quarry and Colliery. This supports my thinking that the internal line on the map in 1895 was a n.g. tramway. It seems likely however that in 1902 the link had just about been put in but was not yet documented fully.

As the quarrying activities expanded, the White House became relatively less important as a farmstead but, along with its numerous outbuildings and additions, it developed as a centre of vast activity and accommodation during the peaks of quarrying - first encouraged by the Tynemouth Corporation's needs in the Edwardian period and then booming again in the years closely following the end of the first world war ; note, on a later page, that in 1921 sixty-two people from the White House signed a petition calling for the maintenance of Fontburn station. It has been suggested that workers, resident and others, at the quarries totalled over one hundred at that period. Many itinerant workers trekked to White House, some coming from Catcleugh as that job finished around 1904-05.

Mr George McKenna and his sister Miss McKenna, the Fontburn schoolmistress, have reconstructed the scene on that hillside. At the top was Ritton White House itself, in full occupation. 'The Bothy' was one of the farm buildings and occupied by Irish navvies. The Catholic church was adapted from a barn. Below these buildings was 'the Club' or canteen, in charge of Mr and Mrs Crosby, who had their quarters incorporated in it. Then there was the mission house (or hall) and, lower again, other living huts, with 'Cockney Row' (five huts in a group or single terrace) at right angles to them; the 'black huts' (no doubt tarred against the rigours of the westerly winds and weather) were the lower ones. Miss McKenna continued to occupy a cosy hut below the White House many years after the residential settlement of the site had declined.

Fontburn Halt and the Rothbury branch of the North British Railway.

The opening of the Rothbury branch railway, in 1870, and its closing to passengers (in 1952) and to all traffic (in 1963) have been mentioned by way of introduction to the Fontburn story. Reference has also been made to the connections into the Railway Company's line of the private sidings of the Whitehouse Limeworks and the associated Ewesley Quarry, also to the siding put in to serve the waterworks but which remained for many years after the Fontburn reservoir had been completed. The Tynemouth Corporation's

The goods yard (left) and exterior of passenger station (right) at Rothbury, also in September 1961. The N.E.R. van is **NOT TO LEAVE ROTHBURY**.

Rothbury station from the extreme end of the former North British Railway branch line, with run-round loop, turntable, locomotive shed, seen in September 1961. The signal box is just hidden at the far end of the platform.

contractor George Lawson inspired the Railway Company to instal the siding, operational from February 1902. A proposition for a passenger station in this vicinity was put to the General Manager of the N.B.R., located in Edinburgh, by Tynemouth's resident engineer, Francis R. Hull, who wrote from 'Tynemouth Water, Font Reservoir'. Mr Hull reported that a number of workmen and their families were already, early in 1902, in residence at Ritton White House, which gave its name to the limeworks and will be seen on our map. The quarry company were extending their works and there was to be major development by the Corporation and their contractor. It was pointed out to the Railway that the nearest station, at Ewesley, could best be reached from Fontburn site or Ritton White House by walking along their line and that the provision of a station on the spot would obviate this trespass and attendant danger; this incentive speeded the debate. The Railway Company's organisation was to say the least inconvenient for dealing with affairs on a Northumberland branch line. The General, Manager W.F. Jackson, was in Edinburgh and so was the Superintendent of the Line, D. Deuchars, but the Goods Manager was in Glasgow and the District Superintendent, J. Philip, was far away in Carlisle; no wonder that there was some confusion as to whether the station would cater for workers travelling to the job or for families travelling from the site and district to Morpeth or elsewhere for shopping and social trips, although it should have been apparent to the Railway officers that their train service was not suitably timed for the first group and their obsession with workmen's tickets was irrelevant.

NORTH EASTERN RAILWAY.

From YORK
ROTHBURY
N.B.

65819 formerly NER 1029 built 1908 by North British Locomotive Company and withdrawn in 1966, class P3 or J27, is preparing its train at Rothbury, 10 October 1963. Observe the handsome NBR signal box and the countryside in which is situated Cragside, the first Lord Armstrong's remarkable creation, National Trust property.

However, by June 1902, the N.B.R. had decided to spend £185 on a temporary platform at Whitehouse. This was built on the west of the line, 6ft wide and about 250ft long. A small waiting shed and booking office was also built and a clock was ordered, but no signals were installed and the station (and the siding connections) were located part way through the electric token section from Ewesley station to Rothbury, although in later days (from 16 April 1941) one electric token covered the entire branch line from Scotsgap to Rothbury as a single section. Owing to the preoccupation of the agent or station master at Ewesley with his blockpost, he was not entrusted with checking of traffic for Whitehouse sidings and this was made the responsibility of his colleague at Longwitton, the station between Scotsgap and Ewesley. Outgoing traffic from Whitehouse, including the reservoir siding, was checked and weighed at Scotsgap, also being invoiced there; presumably there was a clerk at the junction. By December 1902 it was being reported that heavy traffic had already developed at Whitehouse, with no one to look after it, and foreign wagons were commonly going home in the wrong directions. Mr Deuchars was having much difficulty in securing any volunteer for the appointment of 'station master' at Whitehouse. This was not surprising; when George Armstrong was appointed to look after the passenger station and the checking of goods traffic (this last under Longwitton and Scotsgap's oversight) he came from being signalman at Whitrope Tunnel box - surely one of the bleakest spots on the N.B.R. - at the age of thirty years, with some ten years railway service and a knowledge of accounts gained at Shankend and Riccarton, was paid £60 per annum and was neither provided with a house nor an allowance in place of one.

Fontburn Halt, seen 15 July 1952, looking towards Rothbury. The chimneys of Daisy (former NBR) cottages are seen, The gate, left behind the north end of the platform, was in its time used to admit Tynemouth reservoir exchange traffic.

The passenger station was opened from Monday, 12 January 1903, under the title 'Temporary Platform at Whitehouse Siding' and it was described further as a temporary platform for workmen. The trains called at 8.5am and 4.49pm bound for Morpeth, at 10.10am, 3.16pm (Saturdays only) and 7.6pm bound for Rothbury. Even then the General Manager was not long left in peace as a stern letter dated 25 February 1903 from the Board of Trade intimated to him that the Board (the President of the B.O.T. in person?) had seen in 'Bradshaw' that a new station had been opened at Whitehouse and could not trace any prior invitation to inspect it. Messrs Blacklock of Manchester, publishers of 'Bradshaw', were taken to task and agreed to delete the entry, while peace was made with the B.O.T. and Major Pringle came down, inspected and agreed to the opening. By August 1903 Whitehouse was again in trouble as the G.M. was informed that goods traffic was regularly going to Whitehouse in Aberdeenshire, when intended for the Rothbury branch. The platform was renamed Fontburn from 1 May 1904. Later that year £29 was authorised for extension of the office at Fontburn. In due course all the passenger trains on the Rothbury branch were booked to call at Fontburn. In the timetable of 1 October 1906, at the height of the reservoir construction works, the southbound trains called at 8.7am, 11.45am, 4.47pm and 6.17pm (the last Saturdays only) and northbound for Rothbury stops were booked at 10.16am, 3.16pm, 5.29pm (Saturdays) and 7.11pm, this last having a connection which left Newcastle at 5.45pm. The 5.29pm bound for Rothbury on Saturdays and the 6.17pm for Scotsgap had ceased to run by April 1910. The daily goods train, also in 1906-07, was booked out of Rothbury at 10.40am, calling at Fontburn around 11.3am and northbound it left Morpeth at 3.34pm and was due out of Scotsgap at 5.10pm, putting off traffic at Fontburn around 5.48pm. Although Fontburn station survived the departure of the construction workers and their families on completion of the reservoir, it was threatened when the Railway Company was looking for economies in the inflationary days after the first world war. From 2 May 1921 the 5.45pm Morpeth to Rothbury ceased to call at Fontburn, in order to dispense with the lad porter and thus save £85.16.0d per annum. It became known that closing of the station early in October 1921 was in prospect. Mr M. Stephenson of Newbiggin farm wrote to the General Manager on 19 September to represent to him the importance of the passenger service here to folk in isolated locations.

There followed, towards the end of the month, a petition which supported this argument and stated that about 120 children made use of the railway. There were 196 signatories. They included the five McKennas of Coldrife, five Nesbitts from Bull Bush, the four Stephensons of Newbiggin, many residents of Forest Burn Gate, others from Coldside and Hollinghill and no less than 62 folk from Ritton Whitehouse, especially Smiths and Parrys. Mr J. Smith was the manager of the Ewesley Quarry

86 WANSBECK and NORTHUMBERLAND CENTRAL SECTIONS. Oct. 1906.

Up Trains. WEEK-DAYS.

Stations and Sidings	Distance from Reedsmouth	1 Pass.	2	3 Rothbury Goods	4 Riccarton Pilot.	5 Pass.	6 Hexham and Scotsgap.	7	8 Rothbury Goods	9 N.-E. Goods and Cattle Mon. only.	10 Cattle Mon. 8 and 22 Oct.	11 Pass.	12 Pass. Sat. only.	13 Cattle Sat. only.
	Miles Ch'ns	a.m.			a.m.	a.m.	a.m.					a.m.		p.m.
Hexham ... dep.	... ...	7 0	...	...	Goods	...	Goods	...	...	...	...	11 38	...	...
Riccarton Junction ,,	... ...	6 40	...	...	a.m. 10 0	...	a.m.	...	...	...	...	p.m.	...	...
—Reedsmouth Junc. dep.	... ...	7 47	...	...	10 10	11 5	11 15	...	...	...	...	4 30	...	8 50
Broomhope Siding ,,	1 26	...	...	Mixed	...	...	...	...	...	...	...	...	...	...
—Woodburn ... arr.	3 64	7 55	...		10 25	11 13	11 25	...	...	...	...	4 38	...	...
—Woodburn ... dep.	3 64	7 56	...		Stop.	11 14	11 50	...	...	...	...	4 39	9 0	...
Knowesgate ... ,,	10 27	8 11	...		...	11 29	12 30	...	...	...	...	4 54	...	...
—Scotsgap Junc. ... arr.	14 2	8 20	...		...	11 38	12 45	...	...	...	...	5 3	...	9 30
	From Rothbury. Miles. Ch'ns.	a.m.		a.m.		a.m.	Stop.		p.m.	p.m.	p.m.	p.m.	p.m.	Stop.
— | Rothbury ... dep.	... ...	7 50	...	10 40	...	11 28	...	...	...	...	2 0	4 30	6 0	
| Brinkburn ... ,,	2 16	7 56	...	10 48	...	11 34	...	...	...	...	...	4 36	6 6	
| Fontburn ... ,,	6 50	8 7	...	11 3	...	11 45	...	...	...	...	...	4 47	6 17	
— | Ewesley ... ,,	7 56	8 13	...	11 13	...	11 50	...	...	...	...	1 17	4 53	6 23	
| Longwitton ... ,,	9 60	8 19	...	11 23	...	11 56	...	...	...	...	...	4 59	6 29	
— | Scotsgap Junc. arr.	13 4	8 26	...	11 40	...	12 1	...	...	...	...	2 30	5 6	6 36	
Do. dep.	13 4	8 28	...	Stop	...	12 3	...	...	1 15	3 30	Stop.	5 9		When required.
— | Middleton ... ,,	15 2	8 34	...	...	...	12 8	...	...	1 25	3 42	...	5 15		
| Angerton ... ,,	16 42	8 39	...	...	...	12 13	...	...	1 35	4 0	...	5 20		
— | Meldon ... ,,	18 64	8 48	...	...	...	12 22	...	...	1 55	4 30	...	5 29		
— | Morpeth ... arr.	24 15	8 59	...	...	...	12 32	...	...	2 15	4 45	...	5 39		
Morpeth (North-Eastern) dep.	... ...	9 26	...	...	...	1 12	...	...	...	...	...	5 45	...	...
Newcastle (Central) ... arr	... ...	9 54	...	...	...	1 35	...	...	...	...	...	6 30	...	...

No. 3 Up.—Engine and Men turn out at Rothbury at 9-40 a.m. to shunt as required. Takes Wagon ticketed for collection of Spare Sheets on Wednesdays and Fridays. Calls at Longwitton only to work Road Van Goods.
No. 5 Up.—On Mondays conveys One Wagon Live Stock from Rothbury to Morpeth, subject to the Regulations as to continuous Breaks as contained in the Appendix to the Working Time Tables. No 8 Up.—Meets at Meldon No. 7 Down.
No. 9 Up.—Meets at Meldon No. 11 Down.
No. 11 Up.—On Tuesdays conveys Live Stock from Reedsmouth to Scotsgap, subject to the Regulations as to Continuous Breaks as contained in the Appendix to the Working Time Tables. Conveys from Rothbury to Morpeth once a week Rothbury and Newcastle Carrier's Van. Meets at Scotsgap Nos. 11 and 12 Down.
No. 12 Up.—Meets at Ewesley No. 12 Down.
No. 13 Up.—Engine with Guard and Van returns immediately to Reedsmouth.
Special Live Stock Train on Tuesdays from Carlisle to Morpeth.—A Special Live Stock Train will leave Carlisle for Morpeth when required at any suitable hour from about 10-0 a.m., but not later than about 8-0 p.m., working General Traffic on return.
N.B.—When required, the Engine, Guard, and Van of the Reedsmouth Passenger Train will make a special Goods Trip from Scotsgap Junction to Morpeth and back, or from Scotsgap Junction to Rothbury and back, after arrival at Scotsgap Junc. at 11-38 a.m., and will shunt Goods Traffic at Scotsgap Junc. They will also do shunting at Reedsmouth when required.

Down Trains. WEEK-DAYS.

Stations and Sidings.	Distance from Morpeth	1 Pass.	2	3 Pass.	4 Riccarton Pilot.	5 Hexham and Scotsgap.	6 Cattle Mon. 8 and 22 Oct.	7 N.-E. Goods and Cattle Mon. only.	8	9 Pass.	10 Pass. Sat. only.	11 Rothbury Goods ex. Sat.	12 Rothbury Go'ds Sat. only.	13	14 Pass.
	M. C.			a.m.	a.m.	p.m.	p.m.	p.m.		p.m.	p.m.	p.m.	p.m.		p.m.
Newcastle (Central) ... dep.	... ...	...	...	8 18	Goods	Goods	...	...	...	1 30	...	...	...	...	5 45
Morpeth (North-Eastern) arr.	... ...	...	...	9 4	a.m.	p.m.	...	...	...	2 18	...	...	...	...	6 7
				a.m.						p.m.					p.m.
— | Morpeth ... dep.	... ...	...	...	9 25	...	...	1 40	...	...	2 25	...	3 45	3 45	...	6 20
— | Meldon ... ,,	5 31	...	...	9 38	...	...	2 10	...	...	2 38	...	4 10	4 10	...	6 33
| Angerton ... ,,	7 53	...	...	9 44	...	...	2 25	...	...	2 44	...	4 20	4 20	...	6 39
| Middleton ... ,,	9 13	...	...	9 49	...	...	...	...	...	2 49	...	4 30	4 30	...	6 44
— | Scotsgap Junc. arr.	11 11	...	...	9 55	...	...	2 35	...	...	2 55	...	4 40	4 40	...	6 50
Do. dep.	11 11	...	...	9 57	...	...	12 20	Stop.	...	2 57	5 10	5 10	5 25	...	6 52
| Longwitton ... ,,	14 35	...	...	10 6	...	...	...	...	...	3 6	5 19	5 25	5 40	...	7 1
— | Ewesley ... ,,	16 39	...	...	10 12	...	...	12 40	...	...	3 12	5 25	5 34	6 25	...	7 7
| Fontburn ... ,,	17 45	...	...	10 16	...	...	...	...	...	3 16	5 29	5 48	6 39	...	7 11
| Brinkburn ... ,,	21 79	...	...	10 28	...	...	...	...	...	3 28	5 40	5 58	6 49	...	7 23
— | Rothbury ... arr.	24 15	...	...	10 35	...	...	1 0	...	...	3 35	5 45	6 10	7 0	...	7 30
—Scotsgap Junc. ... dep.	11 11	...	...	10 7	1 30	...	...	...	...	8 0	...	Stop.	...	...	6 55
Knowesgate ... ,,	14 66	...	...	10 18	2 0	...	...	...	...	3 11	...	...	...	...	7 6
—Woodburn ... arr.	21 29	...	...	10 31	2 20	...	...	...	...	3 24	...	...	...	...	7 19
—Woodburn ... dep.	21 29	...	...	10 32	11 40	2 35	...	...	...	3 25	...	...	...	...	7 20
Broomhope Siding ,,	23 67	...	...	...	11 55	...	...	...	...	...	...	...	...	...	...
—Reedsmouth Junc. arr.	25 13	...	...	10 40	12 5	2 50	...	...	...	3 33	...	...	...	...	7 28
Riccarton Junction arr.	... ...	...	...	1 41	...	...	...	...	...	6 24	...	...	...	...	...
Hexham ... ,,	... ...	...	...	11 43	...	...	...	...	...	...	...	...	...	...	8 38

No. 3.—Conveys Live Stock occasionally from Morpeth to Rothbury or elsewhere, subject to Regulations as to Continuous Breaks as contained in the Appendix to the Working Time Tables. Conveys from Scotsgap to Rothbury once a week Reedsmouth and Rothbury Carrier's Van. No. 7.—Meets at Meldon No. 8 Up. No. 9.—Down is run on to Bellingham.
No. 9 Down.—On Mondays conveys Live Stock from Morpeth to Woodburn, subject to Regulations as to Continuous Breaks as contained in the Appendix to the Working Time Tables.
No. 11 Down.—It is important that this Train gets a punctual start from Morpeth to enable it to reach Rothbury at booked time. Takes Wagon for collection of Spare Sheets between Morpeth and Scotsgap on Tuesdays and Thursdays. Calls at Middleton only to work Road Van Goods. *Meets at Meldon No. 9 Up, and at Scotsgap No. 11 Up.*
No. 12 Down.—*Meets at Scotsgap Junction No. 11 Up, and at Ewesley No. 12 Up.*
No. 14 Down.—This Train must not be kept later than 7-0 p.m. for N.-E. Railway Co.'s Trains from North or South. Conveys Live Stock when required from Scotsgap to Reedsmouth, subject to the Regulations as to Continuous Breaks as contained in the Appendix to the Working Time Tables; also conveys from Scotsgap to Reedsmouth once a week Rothbury and Reedsmouth Carrier's Van.

Working timetable of the North British Railway's Wansbeck and Northumberland sections, 1 October 1906. The Halt at Fontburn achieved that name from 1 May 1904.

Company Limited, who by this time were on record as whinstone and limestone quarry owners and colliery proprietors, registered address Guildhall Chambers, Sandhill, Newcastle upon Tyne. In fact, the station closed to passengers from 3 October 1921 but early in November a visit was paid by C.H. Stemp, whose appointment was by then styled Operating Superintendent and who agreed to reopen the platform from 21 November, but as a 'Halt'. All passenger trains were to call, tickets being issued by the guards and also at Scotsgap and Morpeth. The nameboard was altered to read 'Fontburn Halt', three long-burning lamps were supplied and there was no staff, the station master at Ewesley being placed in charge. From 2 January 1922 Fontburn was closed to goods but Font siding (the one put in first for the waterworks) and Whitehouse sidings (for Ewesley Quarry Company) remained in use and along with Forestburn siding (which had been put in, near the Crown and Thistle Inn, for the by now defunct Forestburn Colliery Company who operated their second-hand locomotive WINGATE upon it during the first war years) and the siding at Ewesley station, they were placed under the station master at Ewesley; his status was raised to 'Agent', with Ewesley regarded as both a passenger and goods station. There had been sidings at Ewesley since 1894. By the latter days of the pre-grouping N.B.R., some attempt was made to provide a business service between Rothbury and Newcastle. The 5.7pm from Newcastle conveyed a through carriage for Rothbury, detached at Morpeth. A regular traveller was Mr F.J.H. Clayton, of Barclays Bank, Newcastle, who resided at Middleton Hall, near Middleton station, which was east of Scotsgap. He was pressing the N.B.R. management, in December 1921, to cut down on the delay at Morpeth, as the Rothbury carriage was booked to stand there nightly from 5.29 until 5.55pm, awaiting connection with a N.E.R. (Blyth and Tyne) train due at 5.42pm. Rothbury travellers were better treated in L.N.E.R. days; for example, in 1935-36, the 5.7pm Newcastle Central to Alnwick 'business train' was first stop Morpeth and the Rothbury carriage was in that station from 5.37 until 5.45pm and commuters reached Middleton North at 6.9pm, Fontburn (Halt) at 6.36pm and Rothbury at 6.51pm, with of course stops at the other intermediate stations too. In the morning the carriage for Newcastle left Rothbury on the 8.12am train and arrival in Central was at 9.45am.

65819, already seen at Rothbury, is approaching Ewesley station, with its Rothbury-Blyth goods on 10 October 1963. Loco coal is being returned after storage (in wagons!) at Rothbury. Font reservoir can be seen in the background. Ewesley itself at the time retained ground frame, siding, platform and house.

George Armstrong has been noted as first station master at Fontburn. The names of Smith, Dick Armstrong and probably Dixon have also been recalled. Mr Hunter was station master at Ewesley for many years, he and his wife occupying the station house. Another Hunter was father of Miss Mary Hunter and he worked on the N.B.R. branch as a platelayer in the era of waterworks construction, the family living then at Daisy Cottages. Miss Hunter's uncle drove the goods locomotive from Rothbury engine shed, making trips to Morpeth and Reedsmouth and retiring around 1937. The bearded Jamieson was driver of the Rothbury passenger engine, in the recollection of Mr George McKenna, the latter onetime of Coldrife and born around the time when the waterworks construction was starting. Rothbury guard Taylor lived at the Mart House, near the station.

Although the Rothbury branch line and its staff enjoyed a passably uneventful career during the first half of the twentieth century, there had been a disastrous incident a few years before the waterworks project was commenced. On Saturday 13 February 1897 an excursion train was booked to return from Newcastle; it left Morpeth that evening well after the last regular train on the N.B.R. and comprised 15 vehicles, Bellingham coaches in front and Rothbury in the rear, with a locomotive working through to Reedsmouth. Rothbury provided 4-4-0 Side Tank locomotive No.72 named MORPETH, with William Burrow, relief driver, and a fireman who had been seven months in the service of the N.B.R. and was on his first trip as a fireman - after dark, be it noted, on a winter evening. They had long to wait at Scotsgap, as the train was very late indeed; it stuck on its way from Morpeth to Scotsgap and they had to go out into the darkness with their engine to find it and couple on ahead of the train engine, to help it into Scotsgap station. After division and departure of the Bellingham portion, the Rothbury engine and men left with 9 four- and six-wheeled carriages fitted with the Westinghouse automatic brake. Tokens were exchanged on the branch at Ewesley. There was then no station at Fontburn and the 5½ miles to Brinkburn, booked 11 minutes, took only 7 minutes, start to stop. Presumably another lively run was made on to Rothbury, 2¼ miles, and that terminal station was approached at 10.21 pm, 90 minutes late. The station master had gone off duty and so had the regular signalman and they had given no operating instructions to either the relief signalman or the relief driver. The signalman failed to check or stop the train at his home signal and, owing to the deficiencies of the station layout and the length of the train, this was admitted by a route via the loading bank line, involving negotiation of hand points, a succession of them, not held by any member of staff. The locomotive stayed on the rails but the leading coaches were derailed. Three passengers were killed and 21 injured, some very seriously. Lieut. Colonel G.W. Addison, R.E., reporting 10 April 1897 to the Board of Trade, was highly critical of the layout and the arrangements, or lack of them. Remodelling and rebuilding at Rothbury, including new station buildings, followed somewhat lethargically and was completed about October 1900.

The Tyers token discussed in the text on the Rothbury branch line. It had earlier been inscribed:
EWESLEY .... ROTHBURY.

APPENDIX

Railways as walkways, and museums of engineering and railways in North East England

I have aimed to convey in my story that, not only has each of the 'temporary' railways for reservoir construction in the 'Northern Dales' had its day, but many of the 'permanent' railways with which they associated have closed to traffic in the last thirty years or so. This represents a loss to the community, social and sometimes commercial too, but enlightened people and local authorities in the North East have saved a great number of routes and adapted them as walkways, cycleways and sometimes bridleways. My friend Mike Ellison has combined his own explorations with the compilation of Rhys ab Ellis ('Railway Rights of Way', published by the Branch Line Society) to provide a table of most such 'ways' in the territory of this book of mine. With slight adjustment by me, this intriguing record is presented. Nearly all the lesser lines of onetime North Eastern Railway and North British Railway which have been mentioned or (to a limited extent) illustrated figure in the table; the Middleton-in-Teesdale branch line, likewise the hill routes above upper Weardale and Stanhope, over Waskerley moors and indeed right through to Wearside. So are Lord Carlisle's Brampton Railway routes (in the main). So is the spectacular Wylam railway bridge over the Tyne (which I illustrate) and the North Wylam branch line - and so are portions of the N.B.R. lines in Northumberland.

Museums

In range, loosely from south to north, one finds Darlington North Road railway museum (S&DR associations, and with the Ken Hoole N.E. archives) and, at Shildon, the Timothy Hackworth museum.

Beamish 'open air museum' (and its archives, and buildings old and replicas) is in the near-Pennine foothills of Durham county - an inspiring creation not to be missed (and allow time in plenty!). Not far away is The Tanfield Railway (locomotive industrial museum and progressively extending operational railway), which allies with the walkway of the same name. Across the county, on the eastern slopes of the Team valley (above the East Coast Main Line) is restored Springwell steam winding engine and associated reconstitution of cross-country colliery railway practice. Wolsingham 'F' pit and Sunderland (Monkwearmouth station) museum sites figure; the latter combines architecture of early N.E. railway days, with content. Tyne & Wear Museums service also offers the Stephenson Railway Museum (located between Backworth and Percy Main, just north of the Tyne), which has created its own railway too - and the central Museum of Science & Industry at Blandford House, 10 minutes walk from Newcastle Central station. Just up-stream is George Stephenson's cottage birthplace (National Trust - beside the North Wylam walkway) and the Wylam Local History Society's collection (prior contact recommended for access).

In deepest Northumberland, the 'high spot' is 'Cragside', created by the first Lord Armstrong contemporary with the high days of his Tyneside engineering and armaments operations - the house and gardens superbly presented by The National Trust - a mile out of Rothbury. The N.T. offer the circuit of 'Wannie Walk' on N.B.R. routes much discussed already and not far away is the Wallington Estate made over by Sir Charles Trevelyan Bart.

Table of 'Railway Walkways' in 'Northern Dales' and neighbouring territories

abbreviations

indus	industrial
LCR	Lord Carlisle's (Brampton) Railway
NBR	North British Railway
NER	North Eastern Railway including Blyth & Tyne Railway

type

track	track - metalled/non-metalled track used by vehicles
FC	forestry commission road/track
FP	footpath
PP	permissive footpath: public allowed to use either at their own risk or restricted times of access (eg not in lambing season)
cycle	trackbed converted to permit use of bicycles
bridle	trackbed converted for use by horseriders, usually requiring a licence from the relevant County Council.

CUMBRIA

Company	Length	Start and End Points		Type
LCR	2.0mls	Tindale Village (NY616592) to Clowsgill Farm (NY589595)	} 2 mls E. from jcn. } for Gairs.	PP
LCR	1.0mls	Clesketts Farm (NY588586) to Forest Head Quarry (NY585575)	} Branch off } Gairs line.	track
LCR	2.5mls	Gairs Mine (NY582555) to Howgill (NY591575)		FP

A panorama of Lambley viaduct, on the former **NER** Alston - Haltwhistle branch, seen from the course of the former Brampton Railway.

other parts of the former Lord Carlisle's railway system are walkable as permissive paths and form a fascinating area to explore.

LCR/NER	1.25mls	Brampton Town (NY538611) to Brampton Junction (NY551600)		FP

NORTHUMBERLAND

indus	1.5mls	Haltwhistle (NY713645) to B6318 Military Road	FP

'Haltwhistle Burn Trail'-history of Blackett & South Tyne Collieries, and much more

NER	13mls	Alston Station to Haltwhistle Station (parts are not walkable, including the Lambley Viaduct over the River Tyne, but it is possible to follow 95% of the former line on the actual trackbed)	FP
NER	2mls	Greenshaw Plain (NY895661) on A69 south to near Bush Farm - part (very limited) of the former NER Allendale Branch	track
NBR	3mls	Deadwater Station (NY603968) to Kielder Station (plans to extend into Scotland to link up with Waverley Route at Riccarton Junct)	FC
NBR	0.25mls	Kielder Viaduct (NY631925) and approaches	FC
NBR	1.75mls	Kielder Dam (NY708881) to Falstone Station	FC/track
indus	1.5mls	Plashetts Colliery Incline (NY674901) off NBR Border Counties line to (NY694907 or near) called the 'North Haul Road'	FC/track
NER	1 mile	A197 (NU295883) to site of Newbiggin Station	FP
NBR	3.5mls	Chesters Burn (NZ011871) on Woodburn line to Scots Gap Station and onto Delf Burn (NZ035885) (on Rothbury line) part of National Trust Wannie Line Walk, open from 1 June to 31 October only.	PP
NER	4.25mls	Wylam Bridge (former railway over Tyne) (NZ110642) to North Wylam Station. and via Stephenson's Cottage (NZ127650) to Newburn Country Park (NZ163655) (once landscaping etc has finished, this should be extended to Scotswood and Newcastle)	FP
NER/ indus.	2.5mls	Ponteland Station (NZ164727) to Darras Hall (NZ144713) then onto former Kirkheaton Colliery Railway to Dissington Road Crossing (NZ136726) - again plans to extend this footpath further westwards towards the former colliery site.	FP

TYNE & WEAR

Prior to the dissolution of Tyne & Wear County there was an ambitious plan to create a long distance footpath, following the former 'county' boundary called the Heritage Way - that would include many former railway lines and waggonways. Several of these lines cross into the neighbouring counties of Durham and Northumberland, but are given here in their full length for ease of reading.

indus	0.75mls	Stargate (NZ163634) to Ryton (NZ168642) part of former Towneley Main Waggonway	FP
NER	10.5mls	Blackhill Station (NZ101523) to Swalwell Station (NZ201624) 'The Derwent Walk'	FP
NER	3mls	Sunniside (NZ209585) to near Dunston (NZ232613) 'Tanfield Railway'	FP/Cycle
indus	7.5mls	Marley Hill (NZ210573) via Bowes Railway to Kibblesworth (NZ245565) and on via Bowes & Pelaw Main Railway to Springwell and Blackhill (NZ279600). Plans to extend westwards to Burnopfield. (Do not confuse with Blackhill near Consett.)	FP/Cycle
indus	2mls	Blackhill (NZ279600) to Allerdene Park (NZ256587), part of Team Waggonway	FP
NER	7mls	Durham, Belmont via Hetton to Murton Colliery (NZ382473)	FP/Bridle
indus	2mls	Hetton Downs (NZ351487) to Warden Law (NZ369513) - historic Hetton Railway, 1822.	FP
indus	4mls	East Herrington B1286 (NZ368530) to Sunderland A1231 (NZ389572) Hetton Railway again	FP/Cycle
indus	2.5mls	Silksworth Colliery (NZ375538) to Ryhope Village (NZ412531)	FP
indus	6mls	Newburn Church (NZ166655) to Black Callerton with branches to Callerton (NZ167691) and Callerton Lane Ends (NZ160691) - part of the former Walbottle Waggonway	FP
NER	3mls	Monkseaton (NZ346723) to near Seaton Delaval A190 (NZ316762) - the former 'Avenue Branch'	FP
indus	2mls	Holywell (NZ319749) to Seaton Sluice (NZ338760) - former Seaton Sluice Waggonway	FP
NER	3mls	Shiremoor (NZ311712) to Percy Main (NZ336673) part of former Blyth and Tyne Route down to Whitehill Point - route follows former BR/Industrial Complex from Middle Engine Lane to Percy Main	FP/Cycle
NER	2.25mls	Rising Sun Colliery (NZ295682) to Middle Engine Lane (NZ326689) former BR line to Rising Sun Colliery	FP/Cycle

indus		Associated with these lines, parts of the former Killingworth Waggonway, Seaton Burn, Cramlington and Backworth Railway systems in this area have been converted into footpaths. eg	
	1 mile	Battle Hill (NZ309685) to A191 Benton Hypermarket (NZ296696)	FP
	6mls	Brunton (NZ215718), Wideopen (NZ242723) and Burradon (NZ270722) to Backworth (NZ299728)	FP/Cycle

The residual councils after the dissolution of Tyne & Wear continue to develop the conversion of former Waggonways and Railways into footpaths, including plans for the former NER Riverside Route on the North Bank of the Tyne, the South Tyne Cycleway from Blaydon via Dunston to Gateshead and the former line on the North Bank of the River Wear from Washington via Hylton to Sunderland.

COUNTY DURHAM (INCLUDING CLEVELAND NORTH OF THE TEES)

County Durham is a mecca of long distance railway paths, with the former network centred round Consett now totally converted into footpaths and cycle paths. Nowadays the impetus has been taken over by Sustrans Ltd who continue the pioneering work of the County Council.

NER	22mls	Consett to Sunderland via Stanley, and Washington - 'The Consett to Sunderland Railway Path'.	FP/Cycle/Bridle
NER	14mls	Consett to Durham (Relly Mill) - a 1 mile section east of Knitsley Station is still subject to a diversion - 'The Lanchester Valley Walk'.	FP/Cycle/Bridle
NER	14mls	Consett via Hownes Gill and Waskerley to Crawleyside (North of Stanhope) 'The Waskerley Way'.	FP/Cycle Bridle
indus	14mls	Parkhead (on Waskerley Way) via Bolts Law to Rookhope and thence via Bishop Seat and Heights Quarry to Westgate in Weardale.	FP
NER	9.5mls	Durham (Relly Mill) to Bishop Auckland 'The Bishop Brandon Walk'.	FP/Cycle/Bridle
NER	9 mls	Durham (Relly Mill) to near Crook, part still closed waiting reclamation of former open cast workings - 'The Dearness Way'.	FP/Cycle/Bridle
NER	7.5mls	Barnard Castle vicinity to Middleton in Teesdale - 'The Tees Valley Walk'.	FP
NER	8mls	Bishop Auckland (adjacent to By-Pass bridge under BR line) to Spennymoor and Ferryhill A167 - 'The Auckland Walk'.	FP
NER	9mls	Hart Station (north of Hartlepool) to Haswell via Castle Eden - 'The Hart to Haswell Walkway'	FP
NER	10mls	From near Wingate to Thorpe Thewles and Stockton 'The Castle Eden Walkway' and also the 'Stockton Cyclepath'	FP

other paths include

indus	0.5mls	Durham Houghal Colliery (NZ288410) a nature trail discovering a lost colliery village to the south of the city.		FP
indus	2.5mls	(near Chester-le-Street) Pelton Fell (NZ253516) southwards via Walldridge to Edmondsley - it is possible to continue on to Sacriston (and Witton Gilbert)		FP
indus	6mls	Whitwell (NZ309405) to Cassop Colliery (NZ343383)		FP
indus	3mls	Near Murton Colliery (NZ395460) to Seaham - the former Cold Hesledon Incline of the NCB system. (historic South Hetton Coal Company route).		FP
NER	16mls	Bishop Auckland to Barnard Castle (undergoing conversion at present)		FP
NER	1.5mls	Cornforth (NZ305345) to Coxhoe (NZ317362)		FP
NER	1.5mls	From A167 part of former NER Newport to Shildon Electric Railway		FP
NER	3mls	Darlington (north) to Dinsdale along original route of Stockton & Darlington Railway. Also the Black Boy and Brusselton Rail Trails follow the former S&DR route west of Shildon.		PP

The melancholy picture, on the former NBR Border Counties line, on 30th March 1975. The lifted routes to Scotsgap (right) and Riccarton Junction are clearly in use as 'unofficial' walkways

Acknowledgments

I wish to record my appreciation of the cooperation and help received in course of my research for this work, whether 'trekking' on the ground or in back-up offices, libraries and journals, and from photographers among names below. I apologise for any omissions below but seek to mention those helpers met and sources drawn upon in the last thirty-odd years. They include, among others - E.L. Ahrons, Kenneth Allderidge, George Alliez, C. Alex Appleton, Mr Appleton (of Hartlepools), Bob Armstrong, J.W. Armstrong; Allan C. Baker, Harold L. Beadle, Jack Beattie, Bob Bowman, Mrs Bowman, J.I.C. Boyd, Jack Bradley, Vic J. Bradley, Laurie Bridgewater, Mr Brodie and fellow farmers on Rede estate, Arthur Brown, Joe Brown, W.A. Brown; W.A. Camwell (for long editor of the Journal of the SLS), George Carter, Les G. Charlton, Ronnie Charlton (of the Redesdale Society), Doug Clayton (of Castle Carrock), R.N. Clements, J.E. Collinson, Joe Crosby; John B. Dawson, Jack Diggle, Tom Dowson; Mr Espin; John Foster, Ian Futers; Brian Gent, Fred Gregory; Thomas Hall, Mr Henderson (of Rochester, Northumberland), Willie Hennigan, Mr Hindmarsh, Clive Holden, Peter Holmes, Kenneth Hoole, T. Hope and Mrs Hope, Richard Horne, Geoffrey Horsman, A.S. Hughes, Hugh C. Hughes, Oliver Humble, Miss Mary Hunter; Jonathan P. James, Kit Johnson, Frank Jones, W.E. Jones; Kenneth Lawson, Paul Lefevre, Peter Lisle; A. Neil Mackay, George McKenna, Miss Nance McKenna, Mrs Margaret Mellon, Tom Middlemiss, E.A. Morris, Paul Mullen, Mrs Murray (Coldtown); Andrew Neale, Mrs Nesbitt, Ken A.C.R. Nunn; Angus Parker, Fred Peadon, John Peadon, Tom R. Pearce, Mr & Mrs Percival (Fontburn), L.R. Perkins, Denis R. Perriam; Alan Richards, Bernard Roberts, G Robinson, Jacob Robson and Miss Phyllis Robson, Eric Robson, Peter Robson (Selkirk), Ralph T. Russell, Mr & Mrs E.G. Rutherford; Mr Sanderson (of Crookfoot), C.A. Serpell, Mrs Jack Shipman and Miss Shipman, George Smith, E.E. (Teddy) Smith, Frank D. Smith, Richard (Dick) Smith, Rick Stewart, George Stobie, Michael Swift; Jack Telfer, W. Telford, Joe Thompson, the Misses Thompson (Castle Carrock), C.H.A. Townley; Arthur Wannop, George Waters, John Watt, Russell Wear, Michael W. Wheeler, Ralph Whitfield, Norman Wilkinson, Mr Wilson (Geltsdale), W.S. Wolfe, Chris Woolstenholmes, Perce Wright and Mrs Wylie (Ridsdale).

Public authorities and companies:

British Railways Board;

Tees Valley Water Board;

Durham County Water Board;

Northumbrian Water Authority (Wear Division);

Hartlepools Water Company/Hartlepool Gas & Water Company;

Sunderland & South Shields Water Company;

Newcastle & Gateshead Water Company (including S.G. Barrett, Mr Irwin, R.W. Rennison and John Ritson, at headquarters);

the Corporation of Tynemouth and (by 1980) the Northumbrian Water Authority at Cramlington (mentioning additionally U.T. Burston, Ian W. Donald, Don Howie, Ian McMillan, Nick Roberts, Jim Sopwith).

Libraries and Record offices:

Beamish Museum: archives and library;

Carlisle city libraries (including John S. Smith, Cumbria county librarian, Mr Wilkinson and Stephen White); and museum (Guy Paule);

Cumbria county record office at the Castle, Carlisle (special thanks);

Durham County Hall (archivist and reference librarian);

Northumberland county record office at Gosforth Park;

Tyne & Wear archives at North Shields (R.G. Durack);

Cleveland county libraries at Hartlepool (Miss M.E. Hoban);

Scottish record office at West Register House, Edinburgh (George Barbour, James D. Galbraith, Colin Johnston).

Published works, including:

Excursion to the Hury Reservoir (W. Gunn/James Mansergh, 30 June 1885)

The Construction of Burnhope Reservoir, Wearhead (Stanley S. Allderidge)

The Railways of Weardale (Tom E. Rounthwaite, RCTS, 1965)

Description of Works (Durham County Water Board, 1959)

History of the Hartlepool Gas & Water Company (Company leaflet)

Lord Carlisle's Railways (Brian Webb and David A. Gordon, RCTS, 1978)

Typescript manuscript on Castle Carrock project (H.L. Groves, in Carlisle library)

Navvyman (Dick Sullivan, from his father, 1983)

Water to Tyneside (R.W. Rennison, 359pp, 1979)

The Impounding Reservoirs of the Newcastle & Gateshead Water Company, 1845 to 1905 (R.W. Rennison to the Newcomen Society, 34pp., November 1982)

The Wansbeck and Northumberland Central Lines 100 years ago (G.W.M. Sewell, N.B.R. Study Group, Journal 32 of 1987)

Paper on Fontburn project (Francis R. Hull, resident engineer)

Notes on Fontburn project (John F. Smillie, onetime Borough Treasurer, Tynemouth, 1 November 1897)

The Font Reservoir Works for the water supply of Tynemouth (from *Water* 1906, pp 9-16)

The Exide Company's house journal, extract

Various issues of *Building News* (courtesy Frank Jux)

The Industrial Locomotive (Industrial Locomotive Society's journal)

The Journal of the Stephenson Locomotive Society (including the present author's papers presented October 1963 and June 1973)

The North Eastern Railway Association

The North British Railway Study Group

Various *Minutes* and *Acts of Parliament*

Arthur Chambers collaborated in the field and at his desk, preparing the maps here reproduced, apart from the end-cover map, which has been based on the author's sketch and prepared by cartographer David H. Smith. Audrey Halsall has transcribed various manuscripts. Douglas Rendell and Dianne have undertaken photographic copywork and the like for the author.

H.D.B.

(N.B. The author and publisher regret that copies of photographs featured in the book cannot be supplied to individuals.)

LESSER RAILWAYS OF BOWLAND FOREST AND CRAVEN COUNTRY
AND THE DAM BUILDERS IN THE AGE OF STEAM

This book - third in the 'Dam Builders in the Age of Steam' chronology - tells the remarkable story of men and machines engaged in the construction of dams and reservoirs in much of Lancashire and Yorkshire during the period from the 1890's to the 1930's. The ground covered is that superb area of Lancashire between the Ribble and the Lune, bounded on the west by the Lancaster - Carlisle Railway, extending eastwards into Yorkshire, touching the Leeds - Settle - Carlisle railway at Long Preston and Hellifield. The tale then passes into the Craven district of Yorkshire, around Skipton and towards Haworth, of Bronte fame and the Keighley & Worth Valley Railway.

Following an outline of the historical background to each scheme, the author describes the often complex railway systems developed by the Water Authorities (or their chosen Contractors) to service the construction works. Daily life on the railways is chronicled as they carry earthfill material to the dam site, clay from the clayfields, stone from the quarries, bricks and cement, and coal for locomotives and other steam plant. To isolated navvy settlements they provide and all-round transport service, for mail, groceries, beer and clothing, and many railways are used for man-riding by the 'paddy mail' train morning and evening. Railways of 3ft. gauge predominate, but 2 ft. and 4 ft. 8½ in. gauges also appear.

The author has identified more than 80 locomotives from builders such as Bagnall, Andrew Barclay, Hunslet, Hudswell Clarke, Kerr Stuart, Manning Wardle, Peckett, Sentinel and Motor Rail and describes these - listing their dates, makers' numbers etc. He delves back into the often obscure origins of locomotives secured from earlier owners, and also sketches in their careers subsequent to the job in hand.

Readers who know the author, his work and writings in the fields of industrial and main line railway history and operation will expect highly authentic material, coupled with concise but literary presentation - and plenty of anecdote and incident too. They will not be disappointed. Harold Bowtell likes to tramp his sites and railway routes, and for over thirty years he has been seeking out old hands who can recall the days of hard-pressed activity by men and their little locomotives, steam navvies (excavators) and traction engines too. In addition he has delved deeply into the records of Water Authorities, locomotive builders, archives, libraries and professional sources. Cartographer Arthur Chambers has joined in site visits and studied old photographs in order to reconstruct in thirteen maps and diagrams the changing railway and plant layouts: these maps will be particularly valuable to those wishing to search out and explore visible remains of these fascinating forgotten railways. The narrative is complemented by 75 black and white photographs (many previously unpublished) and the dust jacket carries a full colour illustration from a watercolour by Roy Link.

LESSER RAILWAYS OF BOWLAND FOREST AND CRAVEN COUNTRY
ISBN 0 9511108 8 8 9½ in. by 6½ in. approx. 112 pages, 13 maps, 75 illustrations,
is published in a casebound edition with full colour dust jacket at £12.95

LESSER RAILWAYS OF THE YORKSHIRE DALES

AND THE DAM BUILDERS IN THE AGE OF STEAM

In his previous three volumes in the series, Harold Bowtell has set out the story of men and machines - with railways prominent - engaged in constructing dams and forming reservoirs among the Pennine hill country of Lancashire and Yorkshire - to as far north as Haworth and 'Bronte land.' Now in this fourth volume, he takes the reader yet further out into the Yorkshire Dales. He explores and brings to life the exciting water-impounding projects undertaken for the people of Leeds, Bradford and Harrogate between mid-nineteenth Century and the present day.

Emphasis is given to the 2ft (and indeed 3ft) gauge railways which, for some 30 years into the 20th Century, linked the North Eastern Railway's Masham branch line with remote Colsterdale - in superb country north west of Ripon. Narrow gauge locomotives by builders from Yorkshire and elsewhere, even unique German machines for work in tunnels under the hills, are located, described and illustrated at their tasks. Incidents are many, and there are spectacular disasters too. The village created in Colsterdale for the workers is also linked with the 'Leeds Pals' and their tragedy on the Somme. The tale touches on the Kirkby Malzeard Light Railway (who has heard of that?), and within the city and suburbs of Leeds an enterprising (nocturnal?) use of electric street tramways is revealed.

Discussion of Bradford's waterworks soon brings the writer to nearly 50 years of railways in upper Nidderdale - again beyond the reach of the N.E.R. Miles of track on 3ft gauge, as well as on 4ft 8½in standard gauge, are discussed. It emerges that Bradford's celebrated Nidd Valley Light Railway was shorter in years and miles than the railways put down by the City's contractors, and in many ways subsidiary to them. This is further brought home when the locomotives of the contractors are for the first time distinguished from those of the City.

Throughout the book, Harold Bowtell's years of delving, not just among academic original sources, but also among the 'old hands' who appear in the pages, bring the engines, men and scenes to the reader's fireside. There are glimpses too of the earlier careers, and later wanderings, of the many locomotives. Maps by Arthur Chambers and an imaginative cover by Michael Blackmore complement the text and the many other 'vintage' illustrations many from private sources and published here for the first time. This work will delight the industrial archaeologist, local historian, citizen of the town and countryside involved, and of course the many devotees of industrial and narrow gauge railways.

LESSER RAILWAYS OF THE YORKSHIRE DALES
ISBN 1 871980 09 7, 9½in by 6½in approx, 160 pages, 11 maps, 124 b/w photographs, is published in a casebound edition, with illustrated dust jacket, at £19.95.